PENGUIN BOOKS

The
DECLARATION OF INDEPENDENCE
and the
UNITED STATES CONSTITUTION

RICHARD BEEMAN, the John Welsh Centennial Professor of History Emeritus at the University of Pennsylvania, has previously served as the Chair of the Department of History, Associate Dean in Penn's School of Arts and Sciences, and Dean of the College of Arts and Sciences. He serves as a trustee of the National Constitution Center and on the center's executive committee. Author of seven previous books, among them *The Penguin Guide to the United States Constitution* and *Plain, Honest Men: The Making of the American Constitution*, Professor Beeman has received numerous grants and awards, including fellowships from the National Endowment for the Humanities, the Rockefeller Foundation, the Institute for Advanced Study at Princeton, and the Huntington Library. His biography of Patrick Henry was a finalist for the National Book Award.

The

DECLARATION OF

INDEPENDENCE

and the

UNITED STATES

CONSTITUTION

ANNOTATED WITH AN INTRODUCTION BY
RICHARD BEEMAN

SERIES EDITOR
RICHARD BEEMAN

PENGUIN BOOKS

PENGUIN BOOKS

Published by the Penguin Group

Penguin Group (USA) Inc., 375 Hudson Street, New York, New York 10014, U.S.A.

Penguin Group (Canada), 90 Eglinton Avenue East, Suite 700, Toronto, Ontario, Canada M4P 2Y3 (a division of Pearson Penguin Canada Inc.)

Penguin Books Ltd, 80 Strand, London WC2R 0RL, England

Penguin Ireland, 25 St Stephen's Green, Dublin 2, Ireland (a division of Penguin Books Ltd)

Penguin Group (Australia), 250 Camberwell Road, Camberwell, Victoria 3124, Australia (a division of Pearson Australia Group Pty Ltd)

Penguin Books India Pvt Ltd, 11 Community Centre, Panchsheel Park, New Delhi - 110 017, India

Penguin Group (NZ), 67 Apollo Drive, Rosedale, Auckland 0632, New Zealand (a division of Pearson New Zealand Ltd)

Penguin Books (South Africa) (Pty) Ltd, 24 Sturdee Avenue, Rosebank, Johannesburg 2196, South Africa

Penguin Books Ltd, Registered Offices:
80 Strand, London WC2R 0RL, England

This edition first published in Penguin Books 2012

1 3 5 7 9 10 8 6 4 2

LIBRARY OF CONGRESS CATALOGING IN PUBLICATION DATA
United States
[Declaration of Independence]
Declaration of Independence and the United States Constitution / annotated with an introduction by Richard Beeman.
p.   cm.—(Penguin civic classics)
Includes bibliographical references.
ISBN 978-0-14-312196-1
1. United States. Declaration of Independence.   2. United States—Politics and government—1775–1783.   3. United States. Constitution.   4. Constitutional law—United States.   5. Constitutions—United States   I. Beeman, Richard R.   II. United States. Constitution.   III. Title.
E221.U64   2012
973.3'13—dc23
2012020982

Printed in the United States of America
Set in Adobe Caslon
Designed by Sabrina Bowers

CONTENTS

SERIES INTRODUCTION

We introduce the Penguin Civic Classics series by presenting our readers with a paradox. On the one hand, there is an abundance of evidence establishing that the vast majority of Americans, whatever their political differences, have an intense love of their country, believing that it has been one of the most successful experiments in human freedom and opportunity that the world has ever seen. And Americans are similarly united in having a deep reverence for their Constitution, for their institutions of government, and for the system of free enterprise that has been such a powerful engine for our economic growth. Americans see all of these as playing a vital role in making the nation as successful as it has been.

But there is an equally large body of evidence suggesting that Americans' knowledge of their history and of the way in which their institutions have worked over the course of that history is embarrassingly meager. For example, a third of Americans believe that the Declaration of Independence was written after the end of the Civil War, and fewer than half can identify the three branches of our federal government. Nearly 40 percent of the students at fifty-five of America's elite colleges and universities could not place the Civil War in the correct half century, and fewer than half of them, when presented with the text of the Gettysburg Address, were able to identify it. Nor does it appear that our knowledge improves much as we move closer to the present. Another survey has revealed that more than half of high school seniors thought that Italy, Germany, or Japan was a U.S. ally during the Second World War, and only 14 percent of those seniors could name any relevant fact about U.S. involvement in the Korean War. As the distinguished historian David McCullough has lamented, "While the clamorous popular culture races on, the American past is slipping away, out of sight and out of mind. We are losing our story, forgetting who we are and what it's taken to come this far."

With these discouraging results in front of us, it is no wonder that there is a growing clamor for an increased emphasis on "civic education," defined by one leading authority as "the cultivation of the virtues, knowledge, and skills" necessary for carrying out one's role as a citizen. That very phrase, "civic education," sounds to many like a doctor's prescription: "You need to take your medicine! It may not be very pleasant, but it is something you need to do in order to ensure not only your own health, but also the health of the body politic." It is our hope that reading these volumes in the Penguin Civic Classics series will be much more pleasant than taking medicine, for although these volumes will indeed help improve the reader's civic *knowledge*, we also hope that they will provide some civic *inspiration*—a genuine appreciation for, even an excitement about, some of the words, ideas, and actions that have shaped American society and government since the nation's founding.

The history represented in these volumes, from the founding of the American colonies in the seventeenth century to the adoption of America's Declaration of Independence to Abraham Lincoln's inspiring Gettysburg Address to Barack Obama's inaugural address as the first African American president in American history, is not merely a collection of names and dates to be memorized but, rather, a set of stories to be absorbed and enjoyed. And they are stories that have a real relevance and meaning to our lives today, whether we are debating the nature of America's immigration laws, the extent to which the federal government should be involved in decisions relating to our health care, or, getting even closer to home, whether local schools and school districts have the constitutional right to search a student's school locker.

In these volumes, the reader will encounter nearly all of the central themes in American history, as well as the dilemmas and conflicts that have provided much of the dynamism and excitement of that history.

The central themes and ideas of American public life—democracy, equality, economic opportunity, the role of government in maintaining that delicate balance between public order and personal freedom, and the government's responsibility to protect certain individual rights—have never remained static, nor have they ever elicited uniform agreement among American citizens.

The very first item in Terry Golway's collection of important American speeches is a sermon given by Massachusetts governor John Winthrop, aboard the ship *Arbella*, as it transported the first Puritan settlers to the new colony. In that sermon, Winthrop described the Puritans' mission in Massachusetts Bay as one of creating a "city upon a hill," a model of virtue and purity for all others in the world to follow. But his vision of that society was in some important respects very much at odds with the values that guide America today. In the opening words of his sermon, Winthrop reminded his fellow colonists that "GOD ALMIGHTY in His most holy and wise providence, hath so disposed of the condition of mankind, as in all times some must be rich, some poor, some high and eminent in power and dignity; others mean and in submission." Hardly a prescription for the democratic society that we claim to be today.

Fast-forward 136 years to the promise contained in Thomas Jefferson's Declaration of Independence that "all men are created equal"—a view of society *very* different from that articulated by Winthrop. Jefferson's city upon a hill was to be a nation dedicated to equality and the pursuit of happiness, not to a divinely ordained, inegalitarian social hierarchy. But, of course, in a world in which Africans were enslaved, women were considered legally subordinate to men and, indeed, in which many free white males were denied the right to vote because they did not own the requisite amount of property, Jefferson's promise of equality fell far short of an accurate description of the reality of American society in 1776. Still, words have power, and Abraham Lincoln, for one, knew the power of those words. As is amply displayed in Allen Guelzo's volume containing many of Lincoln's principal speeches, time and time again Lincoln invoked Jefferson's preamble as a pledge that Americans of his age were honor-bound to fulfill, describing the preamble as "the electric cord in that Declaration that links the hearts of patriotic and liberty-loving men together, that will link those patriotic hearts as long as the love of freedom exists in the minds of men throughout the world."

Alas, Americans would fight a horrific, bloody civil war in which more than 600,000 people, slave and free, lost their lives before the nation was able to take the steps necessary to forge the link to which Lincoln had referred. Beginning in December of 1865, with the adoption of the Thirteenth Amendment, eliminating the institution of slavery; continuing with the adoption of the Fourteenth Amendment (July 1868), with its guarantee of "equal protection under the laws"; and culminating with the adoption of the Fifteenth Amendment (February 1870), asserting that the right to vote could not "be abridged . . . on account of race, color, or previous condition of servitude," those ideas of democracy and equality began to be incorporated into our constitutional system. But although those three amendments represented an important step forward, America's struggle to live up to the promise of the preamble was far from over. It took until 1920 for the nation to adopt the Nineteenth Amendment, giving to women the right to vote, and in spite of the guarantees of the Fourteenth and Fifteenth Amendments, the civil rights of African Americans, including the right to vote, continued to be undermined by the actions of individual state governments well into the twentieth century. When Lyndon Johnson, only the second (after Woodrow Wilson) Southern-born president since the Civil War, signed into law the Voting Rights Act of 1965, he too quoted the preamble to the Declaration and ended his speech with a phrase from the anthem of the civil rights movement of the 1950s and 1960s: "We Shall Overcome." And when the first African American president, Barack Obama, delivered his inauguration speech on a cold day in January 2009, he began his speech by paraphrasing the words of Thomas Jefferson's preamble, urging Americans "to carry forward that precious gift, that noble idea, passed on from generation to generation: the God-given promise that all are equal, all are free, and all deserve a chance to pursue their full measure of happiness." Even in 2009 those words were, like Jefferson's, expressions of hope, not descriptions of reality. But they have proved powerful indeed, and they continue to be a dynamic force in shaping the American future just as they have the American past.

Another important theme that emerges from these volumes of Civic Classics involves the age-old debate on how and where to strike the best balance between public order and personal liberty. For most of human history, those who held government power—kings or emperors or czars—usually dealt with that issue by ruthlessly imposing their own definition of what was good for the masses of people whom they governed. When Thomas Paine published his earth-shaking pamphlet *Common Sense* in January of 1776, his primary purpose was to persuade the American colonists to throw off British rule, but one of the key elements in his argument was the notion that while every society needs some form of government in order to provide security and protect the freedom of its citizens, the best and freest societies are those in which government is least intrusive. In Paine's words: "Society in every state is a blessing, but government even in its best state is but a necessary evil; in its worst state an intolerable one." Paine's words struck a chord with his American readers, who were already suspicious of the overly powerful, distant government of Great Britain, and the Declaration of Independence, approved seven months later, reinforced that same theme. The distrust of concentrations of government power—the notion that government, while necessary, must be restrained—is deeply rooted in America's revolutionary past, and, of course, is very much alive today, as we can observe by the vitality of political movements such as the Tea Party.

As powerful as Paine's and Jefferson's indictments of excessive British power may have been, they did not provide the answer to the question of how the independent American nation could create a government that would strike an ideal balance between order and liberty. The men who gathered in Philadelphia in the summer of 1787 to frame a new constitution for their still-fragile independent nation took a giant step forward in providing an answer when they created a governmental system based on the division of power between the individual states and the central government—the system that we now call federalism—and by further dividing power among the three branches of the federal government—in a system that we characterize as one of "checks and balances."

But, as in so many other important ideas in American history, those involving federalism and checks and balances were subject to many different interpretations. Alexander Hamilton, James Madison, and John Jay, in the eighty-five essays comprising *The Federalist Papers*, attempted to address some of the concerns that Americans had about the excessive power of the proposed new federal government and, in the process, provided Americans with enduring insights about government and politics—insights that are still cited by Supreme Court justices in their judicial opinions even today. But Hamilton and Madison, the two principal authors of *The Federalist Papers,* began to disagree about the relationship of the new federal government to the individual states and to the people at large almost from the moment the new government commenced operation. The debate over the way the words of the Constitution should be interpreted, with Madison and Jefferson taking a "strict construction" position, and Hamilton, George Washington, and others arguing for a broader interpretation of the Constitution, has stayed with us until the present day. As readers of Jay Feinman's collection of landmark Supreme Court cases will discover, the Court has spent a significant portion of its time over the years, beginning with Chief Justice John Marshall's majority opinion in *McCulloch v. Maryland* (1819), wrestling with the extent of and limits on federal government power. Nor has that conflict been confined to judicial or intellectual arguments. In the years leading up to the Civil War, Northern and Southern politicians fought ferocious battles over the question of what authority the federal government had to legislate with respect to the expansion of slavery into new territories; once again, the ever-eloquent Abraham Lincoln weighed in on those issues, as is amply illustrated in Allen Guelzo's selection of Lincoln speeches. In the end, of course, it was not words that settled the constitutional argument between North and South but the force of arms. The Civil War was, in some senses, America's greatest civic failure, for knowledge and reason alone were not sufficient to settle the conflict between North and South. But however terrible the toll, it did resolve the paradox at the nation's core—the existence of the institution of slavery in a nation that claimed to be devoted to liberty.

Mercifully, the Civil War was the last occasion in which our differences of opinion over governmental power have resulted in warfare, but the war of words has never ceased. Whether debating issues relating to economic regulation, immigration, or providing and regulating health care, Americans—Republicans and Democrats, Tea Party members and Occupy Wall Street activists—continue to differ, sometimes passionately, on the way our Constitution should be interpreted.

Americans, perhaps more than any other people in the world, have been ardently committed to defending their "rights." Indeed, when most Americans today think of their Constitution, they think not so much about those enumerated powers such as the levying of taxes, the regulating of commerce, or the coining of money that are contained in the main body of the Constitution, but, rather, they think of the "Bill of Rights." In fact, one of the few mistakes made by the framers of the Constitution in 1787 was their failure even to include a Bill of Rights in their final draft of the Constitution, a mistake that was, fortunately, remedied by the First Federal Congress in 1789. The rights articulated in our first ten amendments, including freedom of speech, the "free exercise of religion," freedom of the press, and freedom from unlawful search and seizure, have not only provided the foundation for the freedoms that we so value today but also have prompted some of our most vigorously debated controversies. Readers of Jay Feinman's volume on some of the most important Supreme Court decisions in our history will discover that, in general, the Court's definition of the rights guaranteed in those amendments has tended to widen over the course of our history. But there remain limits on the Bill of Rights protections enjoyed by Americans. For example, the right of free speech has not extended to public protests in which the threat of violence is imminent, and in an era of GPS tracking devices and CCTV cameras, Americans are confronted with new challenges in defining what constitutes an unlawful search and seizure.

The constitutional protection of individual rights has not been confined to those items specifically enumerated in the Bill of Rights. The Ninth Amendment, which says that the "enumeration in the Constitution, of certain rights, shall not be construed to deny or disparage others retained by the people," has been interpreted to include the right of privacy, including the right of a woman to have some control over her health and reproductive decisions. The best-known of the Supreme Court decisions relating to the right of a woman to terminate a pregnancy, *Roe v. Wade* (1973), far from settling that difficult question, has been followed by a series of subsequent Supreme Court decisions seeking to further refine and, in many cases, limit the right to obtain an abortion. The Court's decisions in these areas, far from being legal abstractions of interest only to a few history or civics teachers, have had an impact, and will continue to have an impact, on the lives of millions of women.

This series of Penguin Civic Classics is based on the belief that acquiring a knowledge of America's history and of our rights and responsibilities as citizens is not merely an abstract, academic exercise. *It really matters.* It can make a real difference in each and every one of our lives. And never more so than in the extraordinarily complicated, tumultuous, twenty-first-century world in which we live—a time of rapid, sometimes confounding, change. The historian David McCullough has spoken of the way in which our knowledge of history and of the way in which our institutions of government operate can give us a "sense of navigation, a sense of what we've been through in times past and who we are." It can also *empower* us. If we are familiar with the way in which people in the past have confronted their problems, and if we have a decent understanding of how to make the best use of America's institutions to deal with the problems confronting us in the present, we have a much better chance of being able to control our own destinies. Our opinions of the "correct" way to proceed may not always prevail, but we will at least be participants, not passive bystanders, in the ongoing drama that is the history of the United States. And, perhaps most important of all, it is often personally more rewarding, more fun, to be a participant rather than to be a bystander.

RICHARD BEEMAN

They are the two most famous documents in American history. Millions of Americans, carefully monitored by security guards, have gazed at them in their specially designed light-resistant, titanium-lined cases in the cathedral-like setting of the rotunda of the National Archives in Washington, D.C. Many more millions have at least some vague recollection of seeing them in the appendices of their primary, secondary, college, and university history and civics textbooks. In virtually every public opinion poll conducted on the subject, Americans not only express their reverence for the Declaration of Independence and the United States Constitution, but also a high level of confidence that they are in fact knowledgeable about what is in them. Indeed, many Americans—whether Tea Party members, Occupy Wall Street protestors, or Democratic or Republican members of Congress—feel so passionately about our founding documents that they claim that they and they alone are the true defenders of the ideas expressed in them, and that their opponents are not only mistaken and misguided but, in some cases, downright "un-American."

Yet whatever their reverence or their passion for the Declaration of Independence and Constitution, all too many Americans lack even a minimal understanding of them. A majority of Americans are not able to distinguish between the Declaration of Independence and the Constitution; in one recent survey, 71 percent of Americans incorrectly believed that the phrase "all men are created equal" appeared in the Constitution rather than in the preamble to the Declaration. In another survey, a third of Americans thought that the Declaration of Independence was written after the end of the Civil War. And in a survey of American teenagers' knowledge of popular culture and American history, more American teens could identify the names of the Three Stooges than could name the three branches of our federal government. Worrisome indeed.

But the ability to memorize the precise language of the Declaration of Independence or to recite specific provisions of the Constitution should not be our only standard for judging who is or is not an "informed citizen"; while the annotated versions of those two documents in this volume will serve as a useful reference source for those wishing to know more about the language of our nation's two founding documents, the more important purpose of this volume is to promote a broader understanding both of the historical context in which the documents were created and of the ways in which those documents affect our lives today. Both the Declaration of Independence and the Constitution are indeed *living documents* as well as *civic classics*, and we will all be better, indeed, happier, citizens if we know something about both their history and their present meaning.

DECLARING INDEPENDENCE

Although both the Declaration of Independence and the Constitution were drafted and signed in the same room—the Assembly Room of the Pennsylvania State House—the cast of characters and the circumstances that produced them were very different. In fact, only eight of the fifty-six men who signed the Declaration were among the fifty-five delegates taking part in the deliberations of the Constitutional Convention eleven years later. The men who voted in favor of Richard Henry Lee's resolution for independence on July 2, 1776, and to adopt Thomas Jefferson's Declaration of Independence two days later, were reaching the end of the road of a constantly escalating thirteen-year conflict with their king and the English Parliament over their fundamental rights as Englishmen. Many of those individuals had done everything possible to seek reconciliation with their "Mother Country," voting in favor of independence only as a last resort. As Pennsylvania's John Dickinson had put it: "The first wish of my soul is for the Liberty of America. The next is for constitutional reconciliation with Great Britain." But, he concluded, "if we cannot obtain the first without the second," he was prepared, however reluctantly, to endorse independence. In fact, Dickinson voted against Richard Henry Lee's resolution on July 2, but soon thereafter signed up to fight in the patriot army during the revolutionary war. Still others—John Adams and Samuel Adams, John Hancock, and Thomas Jefferson among them—felt far less reluctant, and had been prepared for the leap toward independence for many months before the epochal decision in July.

The central idea that unified both the ardent and the reluctant revolutionists of 1776 was a fear of the unbridled power of a distant, central government—a government that could, using its own interpretation of the principles contained in an unwritten "English constitution" as its rationale, act capriciously to deny American liberty. More than two-thirds of the space in the Declaration of Independence is given over to a list of twenty-seven specific grievances—a legal indictment cataloging the ways in which King George III had abused his power at the expense of American liberty. If there was any single lesson that those men gathered in the building that came to be known as Independence Hall learned from their experience during the years leading up to the decision for independence, it was that government power was inherently aggressive and dangerous, and that if liberty were to be preserved, one should give to government only the minimum amount of power necessary to guarantee a proper balance between freedom and security in the society at large.

In drafting the Declaration of Independence, Jefferson knew that the American colonists, as well as potential allies around the world, needed more than a bill of indictment against past English transgressions to persuade them to join the common cause of the revolution. The most stirring phrases of the Declaration, the assertion in the preamble "that all men are created equal, that they are endowed by their creator with certain unalienable Rights, that among these are Life, Liberty, and the pursuit of Happiness," have, from Jefferson's time forward, served as an inspiration to Americans to create a better, more just society. Jefferson's words in the preamble served as an official affirmation of the hope offered by the pamphleteer Thomas Paine in *Common Sense*, in which he proclaimed to Americans that they had it in their power "to begin the world over again," the opportunity to "form the noblest, purest constitution on the face of the earth." In fact, Americans in 1776 were not fully prepared to live up to the promise of either Jefferson's words or Paine's optimistic expression of hope, but the ideas expressed in documents like the Declaration of Independence and *Common Sense* have an independent power of their own, and they have served and continue to serve as an inspiration to Americans to work toward bringing the reality of their social and political institutions into harmony with the logic contained in those lofty phrases.

However important the Declaration of Independence may be in articulating the highest of American aspirations, it lacks the force of law. It is entirely an exhortatory document, aimed at justifying America's bold leap toward independence, at inspiring ordinary Americans to join the common cause of the revolutionary war and, perhaps, persuading some of the nations of Europe to offer America some form of aid in their struggle against Great Britain.

Though the Declaration of Independence may have been drafted to appeal to multiple audiences and though it may have used a variety of rhetorical strategies—lists of specific grievances, lofty philosophical declarations of faith, and even invocations of God's will—the document had one essential purpose—a justification of American independence in the name of *liberty*. But it was one thing to affirm a love of liberty, and quite another to create the institutional structures and to mobilize the people of America in a manner sufficient to achieve it. The Declaration of Independence marked the beginning, not the end, of America's attempt to create a new definition of what a nation founded on the principle of liberty really meant.

AMERICA'S REVOLUTIONARY DILEMMA

In the closing section of the Declaration of Independence, Thomas Jefferson referred to "the united States of America" and asked all Americans to pledge their lives, their fortunes, and their "sacred Honor" to the cause of independence. The American revolutionaries knew that some form of union among the aspiring-to-be-independent American states was necessary. But what sort of union? And here came the dilemma. On the one hand, as we have seen, one of the central causes of their revolution was the fear of an overly centralized government imposing its will from afar. Certainly one of the conclusions to be drawn from the struggles against British rule was that if liberty were to be preserved, government power must be limited and closely watched. Yet the imperatives of fighting and winning a war against one of the world's most formidable military powers required an energetic government with the power to compel the states to cooperate in the common cause.

The initial solution to that dilemma was embodied in "The Articles of Confederation and Perpetual Union," agreed to by the Continental Congress in October of 1777 and finally approved by all thirteen states in March of 1781. In fact, the Articles of Confederation was not a proper constitution at all but, rather, a peace treaty among the thirteen separate states. It amounted to little more than a "league of friendship," a form of alliance in which "each state retains its sovereignty, freedom, and independence, and every power, jurisdiction, and right, which is not by this Confederation expressly delegated to the United States, in Congress assembled." Although it gave to the proposed government enormous responsibility—to provide for the states' "common defence, the security of their liberties and their mutual and general welfare"—it denied to that government most of the powers necessary to carry out those responsibilities. The Confederation government lacked the power to tax; it could only "request" voluntary contributions of money from the independent states in order to support the war effort. It lacked the power to regulate commerce among the states—an omission that sometimes caused the states to behave more like quarreling nations than members of a single nation. The Articles of Confederation also failed to provide for a chief executive capable of giving energy and focus to the new government. The representatives in the only functioning branch of the government, the Continental Congress, took their orders from their state legislatures, with one of the consequences being that apathy within the Congress was so great that it would sometimes go for weeks, even months, at a time without meeting.

By the late fall of 1786, the weaknesses of the Articles of Confederation were becoming all too obvious. The Confederation government had run up a huge debt as it attempted to pay for the costs of fighting the revolutionary war; much of that debt was owed to foreign nations like France and Holland, who were not inclined to be lenient to the fragile, and delinquent, American nation. Many of America's political leaders were disturbed by the ways in which the legislatures of the independent state governments were pursuing policies that, though popular in the eyes of the people who elected them, served to undermine the stability of the new republic. Some states pursued financial policies that posed a grave danger to the public credit; others passed laws erecting tariff barriers that impeded free trade among the states; still others passed laws that deprived suspected Loyalists basic rights of due process of law and, in some cases, denied basic rights of freedom of conscience to religious dissenters. Fears about these weaknesses were given frightening expression when, in the late fall of 1786, a discontented group of western Massachusetts farmers, fearful of foreclosure on their farms, took up arms in rebellion against the policies of the Massachusetts state government. Although Americans may have fought their revolution in the name of *liberty*, many of America's political leaders, struggling with the age-old challenge of protecting liberty while at the same time maintaining an appropriate degree of public order, began to fear for the future of their revolutionary experiment.

THE MAKING OF THE AMERICAN CONSTITUTION

The fifty-five men who gathered in Philadelphia in the summer of 1787 were no less committed to protecting liberty than their counterparts in 1776, but their experience in the eleven years after the adoption of the Declaration of Independence convinced them that liberty, unless accompanied by order and by a firm commitment to the protection of individual rights, could easily degenerate into licentiousness. Although Thomas Jefferson had benefited from the suggestions of others in drafting the Declaration of Independence—particularly John Adams, Roger Sherman, and Benjamin Franklin—there can be little doubt that the document announcing America's revolutionary purpose was first and foremost the product of Jefferson's intellect and temperament. The drafting of a new constitution for a new nation would require different temperaments and different talents. It is perhaps not surprising that Jefferson's close friend James Madison, whose habits of mind were more scholarly, more cautious, would take the lead in organizing the effort to write a constitution designed to bind the independent American states together into a single nation. But the making of the American Constitution was not the act of a single individual. A truly successful constitution would depend on the collective abilities of all of the delegates gathered in Philadelphia in the summer of 1787. It would depend on patience, deliberation, conciliation, and compromise.

The delegates who gathered in the Assembly Room of the Pennsylvania State House in the summer of 1787 faced a formidable task. The thirteen "united states" that comprised the American union under the Articles of Confederation seemed at that moment profoundly disunited. Yet somehow, in the space of less than four months, they managed to pull off an extraordinary accomplishment. The Constitution they drafted has proven to be the world's oldest, most durable written national constitution. It has, for most of our history, been successful in striking that difficult balance between the maintenance of public order and security, on the one hand, and the nurturing and protection of personal liberty, on the other. And it has brought remarkable stability to one of the most tumultuous forms of political activity—popular democracy.

But it didn't begin that way, nor was the outcome of the Constitutional Convention in any way inevitable. As we look at the work of the Founding Fathers during that summer of 1787, it seems a wonder that things turned out as well as they did.

Looking back on their work that summer, we can identify a few factors that helped them reach agreement on the difficult issues they were confronting. Certainly among the most important was the quality of leadership among those most committed to strengthening the American government. The ringleader was the thirty-seven-year-old James Madison. Standing only a few inches over five feet tall, scrawny, suffering from a combination of poor physical health

and hypochondria, and painfully awkward in any public forum, Madison nevertheless possessed a combination of intellect, energy, and political savvy that would
mobilize the effort to create an entirely new form of
continental union.

Madison was joined in his effort by a group of delegates from Virginia and Pennsylvania who, in a series
of meetings before the Convention formally began its
business on May 25, combined to concoct a plan not
merely to "amend" the Articles of Confederation
(which had been the original charge given to the
Convention by the Continental Congress), but to set
the proceedings of the Convention on a far more am-
bitious course. The first gathering of these reform-
minded delegates took place on the evening of May
16, in the home of Benjamin Franklin, where dinner
was served in his impressive new dining room along
with a "cask of Porter," which, Franklin reported, received "the most cordial and universal approbation" of
all those assembled. The Pennsylvania and Virginia
delegates met frequently during the days leading up to
May 25, both in the afternoons in the state house itself and in the evenings in City Tavern or the Indian
Queen, to craft an entirely new conception of Continental government.

Franklin's and Washington's presence gave the
group both dignity and prestige, but it was Madison and James Wilson and Gouverneur Morris of
Pennsylvania who provided much of the intellectual
leadership. Wilson, a dour but brilliant Scotsman, was

perhaps the only person in the Convention who was Madison's intellectual equal, and he shared Madison's commitment to creating a truly "national" government based on the consent of the people, not the individual states. Gouverneur Morris was nearly as intellectually brilliant as Wilson; he shared with Wilson a desire for a strong national government, but his personality was very different—more mercurial and more outgoing (particularly when it came to his amorous relationships with women). And he was also more openly contemptuous of the excesses of "democracy." Together these men would forge a radical new plan, the Virginia Plan, which would shape the course of events during that summer of 1787.

By seizing the initiative, this small group of nationalist-minded politicians was able to set the terms of debate during the initial stages of the Convention, gearing the discussion toward not *whether*, but *how*, a vastly strengthened Continental government would be constructed. On the second full day of the Convention's proceedings, May 28, 1787, the delegates agreed to a proposal that would prove invaluable in allowing men like Madison, Wilson, and Morris to move their plan forward. To prevent the "licentious publication of their proceedings," the delegates agreed to observe a strict rule of secrecy, with "nothing spoken in the house to be printed or otherwise published or communicated." In our twenty-first-century world, this manner of proceeding on a matter of such monumental importance would be instantly rejected as unacceptable—untransparent, undemocratic. But the rule of secrecy gave to delegates the freedom to disagree, sometimes vehemently, on important issues, and to do so without the posturing and pandering to public opinion that so often marks political debate today. And it also gave delegates the freedom to change their minds; many was the occasion when, after an evening of convivial entertainment with one another, the delegates would return the following morning or even the following week or month, and find ways to reach agreement on issues that had previously divided them. The rule of secrecy helped make the Constitutional Convention a *civil and deliberative* body, rather than a *partisan* one. It helped make *compromise* an attribute of statesmanship, rather than a sign of weakness.

As the details of the Virginia Plan were revealed to those gathered in the Assembly Room of the Pennsylvania State House, it became clear that it was not a mere revision of the Articles of Confederation but, rather, a bold new plan for an entirely new kind of government—a government with a vastly more powerful "national" legislature, with both of its houses to be apportioned according to population, and with a powerful chief executive, an office entirely lacking under the old Articles of Confederation. It also became immediately clear that, however bold and innovative the plan may have been, there were many delegates in the room who had grave misgivings about some aspects of it. For nearly four months, the delegates attempted to work through, and resolve, those misgivings. Over the course of the summer, the delegates would debate, disagree, and ultimately compromise on a host of issues. The most divisive of those issues—those involving the apportionment of representation in the national legislature, the powers and mode of election of the chief executive, and the place of the institution of slavery in the new Continental body politic—would change in fundamental and unexpected ways the shape of the document that would eventually emerge on September 17, 1787.

THE FOUNDING FATHERS AND FEDERALISM

The delegates haggled over how to apportion representation in the legislature off and on for more than six weeks between May 30 and July 16. Those from large, populous states such as Virginia and Pennsylvania argued that representation in both houses should be based on population, while those from smaller states such as New Jersey and Delaware argued for equal representation for each state. The compromise that eventually emerged, one championed most energetically by the delegates from Connecticut, was an obvious one—so obvious that it was proposed off and on by several delegates almost from the beginning of the protracted debate: representation in the lower house would be apportioned according to population, with each state receiving equal representation in the upper house. In the final vote on the so-called Connecticut Compromise, occurring on July 16, five states supported the proposal, with four opposing, including Virginia and Pennsylvania, and one state divided. James Madison in particular was disconsolate. He was convinced that the compromise would destroy the very character of the national government he hoped to create. Indeed, the next morning Madison and several other large-state delegates met to consider whether they should leave the Convention altogether. But they did not do so. Recognizing the folly of allowing their desire for their "perfect" plan to become the enemy of the good, they acceded to the Connecticut Compromise. And, interestingly, Madison would use his "defeat" in the controversy over representation to fashion an entirely new definition of federalism. In "Federalist No. 39" he defended the proposed new constitution against its critics by praising the different modes of representation in the House and Senate—with the House representing the people of the nation at large and the Senate representing the residual sovereignty of the states—as one of the features that made the new government part national and part federal. No one knew how that new definition of federalism would actually work in practice, and it would remain a source of contention for much of the nation's early history. In this, as in so many areas, the so-called original meaning of the Constitution was not at all self-evident—even to the framers of the Constitution themselves.

CREATING AN AMERICAN PRESIDENT

The debate among the delegates over the nature of the American presidency was more high-toned and, if anything, even more protracted and confusing than that over representation in the Congress. At one extreme, nationalists like James Wilson and Gouverneur Morris argued forcefully for a strong, independent executive capable of giving "energy, dispatch, and responsibility" to the government. They urged their fellow delegates to give the president an absolute veto over congressional legislation. At the other end of the spectrum, Roger Sherman, a plainly dressed, plainspoken delegate from Connecticut who would prove to be one of the most sagacious members of the Convention, spoke for many delegates when he declared that the "Executive magistracy" was "nothing more than an institution for carrying the will of the Legislature into effect." This led Sherman to the conclusion that the president should be removable from office "at pleasure" any time a majority in the legislature disagreed with him on an important issue. (By that same logic, Sherman would have allowed the president to be impeached by a majority of Congress for just about any reason at all.) In the end, it was compromise that once again won the day—the delegates agreed to give the president a limited veto power, but one that could be overridden by a vote of two-thirds of both houses of Congress.

Many—perhaps most—of the delegates thought that the executive should be elected by the national legislature; still others thought the executive should be elected by the state legislatures or even by the governors of the states. James Wilson was virtually the only delegate who came out unequivocally for direct election of the president by the people. He believed that it was only through some form of popular election that the executive branch could be given both energy and independence.

But realizing that his proposal for direct popular election of the president was gaining no favor, Wilson proposed a compromise by which the president would be elected by a group of "electors" chosen either by the state legislatures or by the people of their individual states. The delegates didn't like that proposal much more than they liked his proposal for direct popular election, voting it down overwhelmingly at that point. They voted against some version of the proposal on numerous occasions between early June and early September of 1787, only agreeing to the version contained in our modern Constitution (modified slightly by the Twelfth Amendment) grudgingly and out of a sense of desperation, as the least problematic of the alternatives before them.

It has often been observed that the framers' difficulty in deciding how to elect the president was the result of their misgivings about democracy—their fear that the people of the nation could not be trusted to make a wise choice for their chief executive. In truth, it was not so much that the Founding Fathers distrusted the inherent *intelligence* of the people but, rather, that they had a very clear and realistic understanding of the *provincialism* of the American people. They understood that America's vast landscape, the poor state of its communications, and the diversity of its cultural character and economic interests would make it extremely difficult for any single candidate to gain a majority of the popular vote. How could a voter in Georgia know the merits of a candidate in New York or vice versa? Thus they very quickly cast aside James Wilson's proposal for direct election of president as simply unworkable. The other obvious solution—election by members of a national Congress whose perspective was likely to be continental rather than provincial—was ultimately rejected because of the problems it created with respect to the doctrine of separation of powers: the president, it was feared, would be overly beholden to, and therefore dependent upon, the Congress for his election. The creation of an electoral college was a middle ground, and while many delegates feared that locally selected presidential electors would be subject to the same sort of provincial thinking as ordinary citizens, they reluctantly came to the conclusion that it was the best they could do while still preserving an adequate separation of power between the executive and legislative branches. It was a highly imperfect solution to a real problem, but, in the context of the times, there may well have been no better alternative.

THE FOUNDING FATHERS AND SLAVERY

The delegates' commitment to principles of equality as articulated in the Declaration of Independence was, even in the case of free adult males, a limited one. (For example, most of the delegates supported the imposition of property qualifications for voters in their individual states.) But nowhere are those limitations more obvious than during those instances when the subject of slavery intruded into their deliberations. By 1787 slavery in America was in a state of decline. It remained a significant part of the social and economic fabric in five of the states represented in the Convention, but only two states—South Carolina and Georgia—were inclined to argue for an expansion of America's "peculiar institution." Yet the delegates in Philadelphia failed to eradicate that great contradiction to the core values of liberty and equality on which America had declared its independence. Instead, they enshrined the institution of slavery within their new Constitution.

Although neither the word "slave" nor "slavery" is mentioned anywhere in the Constitution, contention over slavery pervaded the debates on the Constitution throughout the whole of the summer of 1787. It was, for example, impossible to discuss questions relating to the apportionment of representation without confronting the fact that the slave population of the South—whether conceived of as residents or property—would affect the calculations for representation. The delegates argued about the proper formula for representing slaves through much of the summer. The final resolution of that issue—a formula by which slaves would be counted as three-fifths of a person in apportioning both representation and taxation—was a purely mechanical and amoral calculation designed to produce harmony among conflicting interests within the Convention. As many disgruntled delegates pointed out, it had little basis either in logic or morality, but, in the end, the need for a consensus on the issue, however fragile that consensus might be, outweighed all other considerations.

The debate over the future of the international slave trade was in many respects more depressing than that which culminated in the three-fifths compromise. Only the delegates from South Carolina and Georgia were determined to continue what most other delegates believed to be an iniquitous trade, yet their insistence that the trade continue for at least another twenty years carried the day. However troubled delegates from the other states may have been, their concern for harmony within the Convention was much stronger than their concern for the fate of those

Africans whose lives and labor would be sacrificed by the continuation of the slave trade.

Finally, the delegates adopted without dissent a provision requiring that any "Person held to Service or Labour in one State . . . [and] escaping into another, . . . shall be delivered up on Claim of the Party to whom such Service or Labour may be due." By means of that tortured language, and without mentioning either the word "slaves" or "slavery," the delegates made a fugitive-slave clause an integral part of our federal compact. It was the one act of the Convention that not only signaled the delegates' grudging acceptance of slavery but also made the states that had moved either to abolish or gradually eliminate slavery in the aftermath of the Revolution actively complicit in their support of that institution.

THE ABSENCE OF A BILL OF RIGHTS

On September 12, just five days before the Convention was to adjourn, George Mason of Virginia rose and expressed his wish that the nearly completed draft of the Constitution be "prefaced with a Bill of Rights." It would, he said, "give great quiet to the people." But the delegates did not embrace Mason's proposal; indeed, when the matter was put to a vote, after a discussion lasting no more than a few moments, not a single state delegation supported Mason's proposal.

That decision, arrived at hastily and casually, would prove to be one of the most serious mistakes made by the men who drafted the Constitution. When Thomas Jefferson, serving as ambassador to France, received a copy of the completed Constitution from James Madison, he was unable to contain his unhappiness at the absence of a bill of rights. "The omission of a bill of rights, providing clearly and without the aid of sophisms, for freedom of religion, freedom of the press, protection against standing armies, restriction against monopolies, the eternal and unremitting force of the habeas corpus laws, and trials by jury in all matters" was, Jefferson wrote in dismay to his friend, a grievous error.

When the final draft of the Constitution was submitted to the people of the states for their approval, the absence of a bill of rights quickly emerged as one of the most serious objections to the proposed plan of union, and had not many of the supporters of the Constitution promised that they would quickly work to add a bill of rights to the Constitution once the new government commenced operation, it is likely that the document would have failed to gain the approval of the nine states necessary for its ratification. Fortunately, the First Congress of the new government of the United States fulfilled that promise, and, in one of its first actions added that bill of rights, making the "more perfect union" devised by the framers still more perfect. Nor was that the only occasion when the American people, acting through their representatives both in Congress and in their states, sought to further perfect the American union. As readers of this volume will discover, "we the people" have added another seventeen amendments to the Constitution after the addition of the original bill of rights. The United States Constitution, which initially consisted of some 4,500 words on four parchment pages, is now a document with nearly 8,000 words.

"APPROACHING SO NEAR TO PERFECTION"

As the Convention prepared to adjourn, the delegates were hardly of one mind about the nature of the government they had created. But whatever their differences, nearly all of the them, true to their revolutionary heritage, had tried to create a government of limited powers but that nevertheless had the requisite "energy" to do all the things promised in the Constitution's preamble: "to form a more perfect Union, establish Justice, insure domestic Tranquility, provide for the common defence, promote the general Welfare, and secure the Blessings of Liberty." A tall order, especially when they were pledging at the same time to create a government that divided power between the states and the nation in such a way as to allay people's fears of an overbearing central power. As the delegates made their decisions about whether to sign the Constitution on September 17, 1787, there was little certainty among them about how this balancing act would work in practice, but they had at least made a start in creating a framework within which issues of state and national power could be negotiated.

Similarly, most of the framers understood that it was necessary to invigorate executive power, but at the same time they wished to avoid creating anything that resembled the unchecked power of the British king. By rendering the selection of the president independent of the legislature and by giving that president a limited veto power over congressional legislation, the framers were on the whole remarkably successful in both invigorating and containing executive power. Successive generations have debated where the balance point between invigoration and containment should rest, but the framers were at least able to set the general parameters for that debate.

The framers' greatest failure occurred in the area of slavery and race. It is perhaps unrealistic to expect these eighteenth-century men to have moved decisively against the institution of slavery, but they failed to seize the opportunity to take even minimal steps that might have eased the way toward the ultimate abolition of slavery. By creating a process by which the Constitution could be amended, they did provide for a way in which their initial mistakes could be corrected, but since the Constitution required the approval of three-quarters of the states for any amendment to take effect, those states that had a vested interest in keeping the institution of slavery in place had an effective veto power over anything that might substantially threaten it. It would take a bloody, ghastly civil war and the loss of six hundred thousand American lives to affect the kind of constitutional change that would eliminate the most fundamental paradox at the nation's core.

On that final day of the Constitutional Convention, it was left to the Convention's oldest delegate, eighty-one-year-old Benjamin Franklin, to sum up the nearly four months of debate, disagreement, and occasional outbursts of ill temper that had marked the proceedings of that summer. Franklin observed that whenever "you assemble a number of men to have the advantage of their joint wisdom, you inevitably assemble with those men all their prejudices, their passions, their errors of opinion, their local interests, and their selfish views. From such an assembly can a perfect production be expected?" The wonder of it all, Franklin asserted, was that the delegates had managed to create a system of government "approaching so near to perfection as it does."

Franklin acknowledged that there were "several parts of this Constitution which I do not at present approve," but, he added, "the older I grow the more apt I am to doubt my own judgment and pay more respect to the judgment of others." Franklin concluded by asking each of his fellow delegates to "doubt a little of his own infallibility" and step forward to sign the Constitution. In that spirit of humility, thirty-nine of the forty-two delegates present on that last day would take that important step forward and, in the process, move America one step forward in achieving a "more perfect Union." If there is any one lesson that American citizens, and their political representatives, might most profitably learn from the framers of the Constitution, it is that injunction from the sagacious Dr. Franklin: Our own body politic would function more effectively, and with a greater degree of civility, if all of us could occasionally put aside our own sense of "infallibility" and engage in the political process with the same spirit of compromise that guided the founding fathers of 1787.

RICHARD BEEMAN

SUGGESTIONS FOR
FURTHER READING

The classic work on the drafting and philosophy of the Declaration of Independence is Carl Becker, *The Declaration of Independence: A Study in the History of Political Ideas* (New York: Knopf, 1922). An excellent recent account of the larger context in which the Declaration was forged is Pauline Maier, *American Scripture: Making the Declaration of Independence* (New York: Knopf, 1997). David Armitage, *The Declaration of Independence: A Global History* (Cambridge, MA: Harvard University Press, 2007) views the wider implications of the Declaration of Independence.

The starting point for understanding how the Constitution was created and what the framers of that document intended is the extensive notes kept by James Madison during the Constitutional Convention. Those notes, together with many other documents relating to the creation of the Constitution, can be found in Max Farrand, *The Records of the Federal Convention of 1787*,

4 vols., rev. ed. (New Haven, CT: Yale University Press, 1937, repr. 1966). Jack N. Rakove, ed., *The Annotated U.S. Constitution and Declaration of Independence* (Cambridge, MA: Harvard University Press, 2009) presents extensively annotated versions of both the Declaration of Independence and the Constitution. For an even more detailed analysis of each provision and amendment of the Constitution, see John R. Vile, *A Companion to the United States Constitution and Its Amendments*, 4th edition (Westport, CT: Praeger, 2006). For a narrative account of the Constitutional Convention of 1787, see Richard R. Beeman, *Plain, Honest Men: The Making of the American Constitution* (New York: Random House, 2009). See also Akhil Reed Amar, *America's Constitution: A Biography* (New York: Random House, 2005) and Jack N. Rakove, *Original Meanings: Politics and Ideas in the Making of the Constitution* (New York: Knopf, 1996).

An excellent brief survey of the revolutionary era is Gordon S. Wood, *The American Revolution: A History* (New York: Modern Library, 2005). Among the most influential works on the American Revolution are Bernard Bailyn, *Ideological Origins of the American Revolution*, enlarged ed. (Cambridge, MA: Harvard University Press, 1992); Robert Middlekauff, *The Glorious Cause: The American Revolution, 1763–1789* (New York: Oxford University Press, 1982); Pauline Maier, *From Resistance to Revolution: Colonial Radicals and the Development of American Opposition to Britain, 1765–1776* (New York: Knopf, 1972); and Gordon Wood, *The Radicalism of the American Revolution* (New York: Knopf, 1992).

A NOTE
ON THE TEXT

The texts in this edition are based on the transcriptions of the Declaration of Independence and the U.S. Constitution in the National Archives and Records Administration. In some cases, the punctuation in the documents reprinted in this edition has been altered for purposes of consistency and clarity; the eighteenth-century spelling in the original documents has been retained. The annotations by Richard Beeman are reprinted from *The Penguin Guide to the United States Constitution*.

The

DECLARATION OF

INDEPENDENCE

and the

UNITED STATES

CONSTITUTION

THE DECLARATION OF INDEPENDENCE

W hen in the Course of human events, it becomes necessary for one people to dissolve the political bands which have connected them with another, and to assume among the powers of the earth, the separate and equal station to which the Laws of Nature and of Nature's God entitle them, a decent respect to the opinions of mankind requires that they should declare the causes which impel them to the separation.

☞ This single opening sentence of the preamble to the Declaration of Independence displays brilliantly the ability of the document's principal author, Thomas Jefferson, to convey a wealth of meaning in just a few elegant words. It announces the Americans' intention of declaring their independence, of dissolving "the political bands" that had connected them to England. The justification for this extraordinary act was to be found in "the Laws of Nature and of Nature's God." Jefferson, a deist who did not believe that God played an active hand in the affairs of mankind, nevertheless did believe that certain natural laws were God-given. This first sentence also signals Jefferson's awareness that a compelling public statement of the reasons for the decision to seek independence from England was necessary if America's political leaders were going to earn the support not only of the people of their own colonies but, equally important, of foreign nations like France, whose support for the American military effort against England was considered crucial. Before declaring those "causes which impel them to separation," however, Jefferson lays out the general philosophy on which America's quest for independence was founded.

We hold these truths to be self-evident, that all men are created equal, that they are endowed by their Creator with certain unalienable Rights, that among these are Life, Liberty and the pursuit of Happiness.—That to secure these rights Governments are instituted among Men, deriving their just powers from the consent of the governed.—That whenever any Form of Government becomes destructive of these ends, it is the Right of the People to alter or to abolish it, and to institute new Government, laying its foundation on such principles and organizing its powers in such form, as to them shall seem most likely to effect their Safety and Happiness.

☞ The ideas embodied in the powerful opening lines of the second paragraph of the Declaration were not Jefferson's alone. The late seventeenth-century English political philosopher John Locke had written in his *Second Treatise of Civil Government* that "life, liberty, and estate" were among the "natural rights" of mankind; they were rights that existed even before governments were created, at a time when mankind was living in a "state of nature." Jefferson's fellow Virginian George Mason, again following Locke, had included in the preamble of the Virginia Declaration of Rights, penned just a few weeks before Jefferson wrote the Declaration of Independence, "That all men are by nature equally free and independent and have certain inherent rights," which he described as "the enjoyment of life and liberty, with the means of acquiring and possessing property, and pursuing and obtaining happiness and safety." But Jefferson's language has more forceful simplicity. The assertion that "all men are created equal" was in 1776 more an as-yet-unfulfilled promise than a statement of political fact, but it has helped to define some of the highest aspirations of the American nation throughout its history.

The opening lines of the second paragraph were, in fact, merely a preface to the real punch line of that paragraph: the assertion of the right to rebel against the government of England. Jefferson reminds his audience that the very purpose of government is to protect the natural rights of mankind. Since governments, at the time of their creation, base their authority on the consent of the people whom they are governing, then it is also the right of the people "to alter or to abolish" that government if its actions threaten the very liberties it was created to protect. Realizing the dangers of living in a society *without government*, Jefferson was quick to add that once the people had severed their connection with their government, they must move to form new governments whose principles and powers would be supportive of the people's "Safety and Happiness."

Prudence, indeed, will dictate, that Governments long established should not be changed for light and transient causes; and accordingly all experience hath shewn, that mankind are more disposed to suffer, while evils are sufferable, than to right themselves by abolishing the forms to which they are accustomed. But when a long train of abuses and usurpations pursuing invariably the same Object evinces a design to reduce them under absolute Despotism, it is their right, it is their duty, to throw off such Government, and to provide new Guards for their future security.— Such has been the patient sufferance of these Colonies; and such is now the necessity which constrains them to alter their former Systems of Government. The history of the present King of Great Britain is a history of repeated injuries and usurpations, all having in direct object the establishment of an absolute Tyranny over these States. To prove this, let Facts be submitted to a candid world.

☞ The men representing their colonies in the Second Continental Congress had reached the decision to declare independence reluctantly, even painfully. They had a deep reverence for English common law and indeed for the body of law and custom that they called the "English constitution." And nearly up to the moment of independence, many of those leaders expressed great affection for the institution of the monarchy. For all those reasons, the men who endorsed the Declaration of Independence wished to emphasize that their decision was not one arrived at rashly—that they had done everything within their power to find some alternative to the decision to revolt against the authority of the Crown, and that only the "long train of abuses" and the "repeated injuries and usurpations" committed by King George III had driven them to this final, decisive action.

Although Jefferson and those endorsing his Declaration were no doubt sincere in their protestations that independence was only a last resort after all other peaceful means of protecting their liberties had been exhausted, the Declaration's description of the actions and motives of the English king and government is hardly an evenhanded recitation of the facts of the case. There is an element of hysteria—or perhaps of exaggeration for the purposes of propaganda—in the charge that the actions of the king and his government were deliberately designed to "reduce them [the American colonists] under absolute Despotism," or that the entire reign of King

George III, an imperfect but not evil sovereign, had been aimed at establishing an "absolute Tyranny" over the Americans. But given the purposes of the Declaration—to persuade an uncertain American public that revolution was the last and best hope and to persuade foreign nations to give their aid to that revolution—evenhandedness was not Jefferson's highest priority. And so what followed was a long list—taking up more than two-thirds of the whole document—of the grievances that had impelled Americans to take such desperate measures.

[1] He has refused his Assent to Laws the most wholesome and necessary for the public good.

[2] He has forbidden his Governors to pass Laws of immediate and pressing importance, unless suspended in their operation until his Assent should be obtained; and when so suspended, he has utterly neglected to attend to them.

[3] He has refused to pass other Laws for the accommodation of large districts of people, unless those people would relinquish the right of Representation in the Legislature, a right inestimable to them and formidable to tyrants only.

[4] He has called together legislative bodies at places unusual, uncomfortable, and distant from the depository of their public Records, for the sole purpose of fatiguing them into compliance with his measures.

[5]   He has dissolved Representative Houses repeat-
      edly, for opposing with manly firmness his inva-
      sions on the rights of the people.

[6]   He has refused for a long time, after such dissolu-
      tions, to cause others to be elected; whereby the
      Legislative powers incapable of Annihilation
      have returned to the People at large for their ex-
      ercise; the State remaining in the meantime ex-
      posed to all the dangers of invasion from without
      and convulsions within.

[7]   He has endeavoured to prevent the population of
      these States; for that purpose obstructing the
      Laws for Naturalization of Foreigners; refusing
      to pass others to encourage their migrations
      hither and raising the conditions of new Appro-
      priations of Lands.

[8]   He has obstructed the Administration of Justice
      by refusing his Assent to Laws for establishing
      Judiciary powers.

[9]   He has made Judges dependent on his Will alone,
      for the tenure of their offices and the amount and
      payment of their salaries.

[10] He has erected a multitude of New Offices, and
      sent hither swarms of Officers to harrass our
      people and eat out their substance.

[11] He has kept among us in times of peace Standing
      Armies, without the Consent of our legislatures.

[12] He has affected to render the Military indepen-
      dent of and superior to the Civil power.

[13] He has combined with others to subject us to a

jurisdiction foreign to our constitution and unac-
knowledged by our laws, giving his Assent to
their Acts of pretended Legislation:

[14] For quartering large bodies of troops among us;

[15] For protecting them by a mock Trial from punishment for any Murders which they should
commit on the Inhabitants of these States;

[16] For cutting off our Trade with all parts of the
world;

[17] For imposing Taxes on us without our Consent;

[18] For depriving us in many cases of the benefits of
Trial by Jury;

[19] For transporting us beyond Seas to be tried for
pretended offences;

[20] For abolishing the free System of English
Laws in a neighbouring Province, establishing
therein an Arbitrary government and enlarging
its Boundaries, so as to render it at once an example and fit instrument for introducing the
same absolute rule into these Colonies.

[21] For taking away our Charters, abolishing our
most valuable Laws, and altering fundamentally
the Forms of our Governments.

[22] For suspending our own Legislatures, and declaring themselves invested with power to legislate
for us in all cases whatsoever.

[23] He has abdicated Government here, by declaring
us out of his Protection and waging War against us.

[24] He has plundered our seas, ravaged our Coasts,

burnt our towns, and destroyed the lives of our people.

[25] He is at this time transporting large Armies of foreign Mercenaries to compleat the works of death, desolation and tyranny, already begun with circumstances of Cruelty and perfidy scarcely paralleled in the most barbarous ages and totally unworthy the Head of a civilized nation.

[26] He has constrained our fellow Citizens taken Captive on the high Seas to bear Arms against their Country, to become the executioners of their friends and Brethren or to fall themselves by their Hands.

[27] He has excited domestic insurrections amongst us and has endeavoured to bring on the inhabitants of our frontiers the merciless Indian Savages, whose known rule of warfare, is an undistinguished destruction of all ages, sexes and conditions.

The opening paragraphs of the Declaration display the talents of Thomas Jefferson as a literary stylist and a political philosopher. In the list of specific grievances, we see Jefferson the lawyer at work. It is an exhaustive—and wholly one-sided—bill of indictment of British rule in America. On the one hand, there is a monotony to the recitation of each of the twenty-seven grievances, but on the other hand, as the list of grievances accumulates, Jefferson's tone, much like that of a prosecuting attorney delivering his summation to a jury, grows steadily more belligerent, more heated in its sense of outrage at British depredations. Nor is it merely the British actions that elicit contempt; even worse is the British *intent*. The British government and the British king in particular are portrayed as guilty, not merely of bad policies, but also of proceeding with malevolent *motives*. The grievances laid out in the Declaration are not merely *constitutional;* they are also intensely *personal*.

In the years leading up to independence, the colonists directed most of their petitions and complaints at the British parliament. They often prefaced those petitions to Parliament with expressions of their pride and loyalty as British subjects and their affection, even reverence, for both the institution of the monarchy and the person of the monarch himself, King George III. But by 1776, the Americans had reached the point where they were denying that Parliament had any authority over them whatsoever. If Parliament had no authority, then why even waste time addressing that body? Consistent with its denial of parliamentary authority, the Declaration studiously avoids any mention of Americans as British subjects. It speaks of the Americans' fundamental rights as a "people," and it lays the blame for the people's travail squarely on King George III—the "He" to whom most of the grievances refer. This decision to direct their ire at the king rather than Parliament signaled the Americans' intention to affect a fundamental shift in their allegiance, to sever altogether their relationship with their mother country, as represented by the king.

Buried in the long list of grievances—seventeenth of the twenty-seven—is the complaint with which the conflict with England began, and from which nearly all the other grievances flowed: the denunciation of the king "for imposing Taxes on us without our Consent." The American insistence that the British parliament had no right to tax them without their consent provoked the first sustained colonial protests, beginning with the Sugar and Stamp Acts of 1764 and 1765, respectively, and continuing with the Townshend duties in 1768 and the Tea Act in 1773. That this particular grievance appears in the middle of the list suggests how far the Americans had come in their opposition to British control over their affairs. The British attempts to tax the colonies were an important catalyst for what would ultimately become a revolution, but they were only that; the real causes of the American Revolution went much deeper, to the very idea that only Americans themselves could be responsible for their own governance.

There were several grievances that emerged as a direct consequence of the British decision to tax the colonies. The tenth grievance accuses the king of sending "swarms of Officers to harrass our people," an accusation that no doubt refers to the British government's decision to send additional customs officers to America to attempt to collect the new taxes imposed on the Americans. The eleventh grievance condemns the king for sending "Standing Armies" to America "in times of peace." From the British point of view, the troops were sent to aid the customs officers in carrying out their duties and to keep the peace in a situation that, from Parliament's perspective, was growing increasingly disorderly. From the American point of view, however, the decision to send the troops was one of the most ominous, for it raised the specter of military despotism and made an already volatile situation even more so. Adding insult to injury, the decision to send troops to America was accompanied by another parliamentary act that ordered Americans to provide lodging for those troops—the subject of the fourteenth grievance. The thirteenth grievance, one of the most convoluted in the list, charges the king with combining "with others to subject us to a jurisdiction foreign to our constitution." Those "others" were apparently the British parliament, which in the Declaratory Act of 1766 had asserted its right to legislate for the colonies "in all cases whatsoever," and the Board of Trade, which was charged with implementing and enforcing the new taxes imposed on the Americans.

A significant number of the grievances—nine in all—deal with encroachments on the rights of the provincial legislatures of the colonies. The king is blamed for refusing to approve laws passed by those legislatures (number 1); for instructing his governors to prevent laws already passed from going into effect (number 2); for not allowing laws to go into effect unless the people give up their right to representation in the legislature (number 3); for calling the legislatures into session at times and in places that make it difficult for them to do their business (number 4); for forcing colonial legislatures to adjourn and then preventing them from doing their business, against their wishes (number 5); for refusing to call for new elections of representatives, making it impossible for new sessions of the legislatures to begin their business and leaving the colonies without functioning governments (number 6); for refusing to agree to laws establishing provincial courts, thus threatening the colonists' control over their own judicial powers (number 8); for revoking the charters of government under which the colonies operate and, in the process, abolishing their laws (number 21); and, finally, for suspending—and in effect abolishing—some of the colonies' legislatures, thereby depriving the colonies of their right to govern themselves (number 22).

It is not at all surprising that the Declaration of Independence would devote so much space in its list of specific grievances to encroachments on the provincial legislatures. Nearly all the members of the Continental Congress who signed the Declaration were members of those legislatures. They had taken pride in the independence and autonomy of their legislatures— they considered them to be American versions of the House of Commons. But as the conflict with England escalated, royal governors and other agents of the king not only threatened the independence and autonomy of the colonial legislatures but also the prestige and power of the provincial legislators themselves. The Americans viewed these encroachments on their legislatures therefore not merely as *constitutional* threats but also as intensely *personal* assaults on their prestige and dignity.

Several of the grievances deal with the imperial government's interference with American judicial processes: making colonial judges dependent on the British government for their continuation in office and for their salaries (number 9); depriving the colonists of the right of trial by jury (number 18); attempting to transport some colonists accused of crimes back to Great Britain, to be tried there, rather than in colonial courts (number 19); and protecting British troops, "by mock Trial, from punishment for any Murders which they should commit on the Inhabitants of these States" (number 15). This last grievance, which most likely refers to the trial of the British soldiers involved in the Boston Massacre in 1770, was not wholly fair. Although the British soldiers accused of killing five Bostonians in a scuffle were acquitted, they did receive a fair trial; indeed the American patriot leader John Adams stepped forward to defend them.

If the American grievances began with taxation and gradually extended to perceived threats to colonial legislative and judicial processes, still other grievances came to the fore in the years immediately preceding independence; it was these grievances that provided much of the emotional dynamic in the American opposition to British rule. When, in response to the Boston Tea Party, Parliament passed the package of acts that came to be known as the Coercive Acts, Americans faced new, and increasingly ominous, threats to their liberties. The Massachusetts Government Act had the practical effect of replacing Massachusetts's royal government and charter with a military government headed by General Thomas Gage, actions reported in the twelfth and twenty-first grievances, which accuse the king of rendering the military superior to civilian power and of "altering fundamentally the Forms of our Governments." The sixteenth grievance, which complains of British edicts that cut off American trade "with all parts of the world," was a response to the Boston Port Act, which closed Boston's port to all trade until the town's citizens paid for the tea they had thrown into the harbor. The twentieth grievance amounts to a broad-brushed, and somewhat unfair, attack on the Quebec Act. The intention of that act was to take the first steps in organizing the vast territories in Canada that England had acquired after its victory over France in the Seven Years' War. The act made no provision for representative assemblies in that territory—a step the Americans interpreted, or perhaps misrepresented, as a prelude to an attack on all representative government in the thirteen mainland English colonies.

The final five grievances on the list build to a crescendo of outrage over British actions occurring after the outbreak of actual warfare in April of 1775. The twenty-third grievance acknowledges the reality of the state of war but places blame for that state entirely on the king. The twenty-fourth grievance, with its charge that the king has "plundered our seas, ravaged our Coasts, burnt our towns, and destroyed the lives of our people," may have been technically true, for that is the nature of warfare, but it was certainly a one-sided depiction of the growing military conflict between the two sides. The twenty-fifth grievance, which condemns the king for sending foreign mercenaries—German Hessian soldiers—to help the British army fight its war to subdue the colonies, escalates the war of words still further with its charge that the whole aim of those foreign troops was to "compleat the works of death, desolation and tyranny," all carried out in a manner that was "scarcely paralleled in the most barbarous ages." In December 1775, after reading and rejecting the so-called Olive Branch Petition from the Continental Congress, King George III declared the colonies in a state of rebellion, and in support of that declaration, Parliament passed the Prohibitory Act, effectively declaring war on American commerce on the high seas and making any sailor on an American merchant ship liable to seizure and subsequent impressment into service in the British navy. The twenty-sixth grievance, with its lament that the victimized Americans were being forced to "become the executioners of their friends and Brethren, or to fall themselves by their own Hands," once again lays the blame not at the doorstep of Parliament, but at that of the king.

The final grievance in the Declaration's list, the twenty-seventh, is extraordinary in several ways. The immediate source of the grievance was the proclamation of Virginia's royal governor, Lord Dunmore, who promised freedom to any of Virginia's slaves who deserted their masters to fight on the side of the British. There is considerable irony, as well as tragedy, in the fact that it was Lord Dunmore's offer of *freedom* to slaves who joined the British cause that convinced Virginia's slave-owning class that the British were intent on robbing them of their liberties—indeed intent on enslaving *them*. Nor was it the inciting of "domestic insurrections" alone that alarmed Americans. That final grievance goes on to denounce the king for inciting the "merciless Indian Savages whose known rule of warfare, is an undistinguished destruction of all ages, sexes and conditions" to make war against white English colonists. While the king and Parliament were hardly blameless in the matter of inciting Indian violence on the American frontier, the American colonists themselves, by their relentless move westward onto Indian lands, did most of the inciting. And the description of the "known rule of warfare" of the "merciless Indian Savages" is the most shockingly ethnocentric piece of language to appear in any of America's founding documents. Thomas Jefferson, when he penned those words, may have thought that they would strengthen his fellow colonists' commitment to band together to fight the English foe, but the words would bring no credit upon the author.

In his initial draft of the Declaration, Jefferson included one other item in the bill of indictment against
the king. It is extraordinary both in its length relative
to the other specific grievances in the Declaration and
in the passion with which it is articulated. It read:

He has waged cruel war against human nature itself, violating its most sacred rights of life & liberty, in
the persons of a distant people who never offended
him, captivating & carrying them into slavery in another hemisphere, or to incur miserable death in their
transportation thither. This piratical warfare, the op-
probrium of *infidel* powers is the warfare of the *Chris-
tian* king of Great Britain. Determined to keep open
a market in which MEN should be bought & sold, he
has prostituted his negative for suppressing every legislative attempt to prohibit or restrain this execrable
commerce and that this assemblage of horrors might
want no fact of distinguished die, he is now exciting
those very people to rise in arms among us, and to
purchase that liberty of which *he* has deprived them,
by murdering the people among whom *he* also ob-
truded them; thus paying off former crimes committed against the *liberties* of one people, with crimes
which he urges them to commit against the *lives* of
another.

☞ Clearly, the American colonists were not innocent and unwilling victims of British attempts to impose the institution of slavery upon them. And of course Jefferson's own history as a slaveholder—he owned at least one hundred, and perhaps as many as two hundred, slaves at the time he wrote those lines—raises doubts about the consistency, if not the sincerity, of his indictment of British complicity in the slave trade. As things turned out, Jefferson's statement of principle, if that is what it was, did not survive the drafting committee's review. As Jefferson recalled, his condemnation of the slave trade "was struck out in complaisance to South Carolina and Georgia, who had never attempted to restrain the importation of slaves, and who on the contrary still wished to continue it."

In every stage of these Oppressions We have Petitioned for Redress in the most humble terms: Our repeated Petitions have been answered only by repeated injury. A Prince whose character is thus marked by every act which may define a Tyrant, is unfit to be the ruler of a free people.

Nor have We been wanting in attentions to our Brittish brethren. We have warned them from time to time of attempts by their legislature to extend an unwarrantable jurisdiction over us. We have reminded them of the circumstances of our emigration and settlement here. We have appealed to their native justice and magnanimity, and we have conjured them by the ties of our common kindred to disavow these usurpations, which would inevitably interrupt our connections and correspondence. They too have been deaf to the voice of justice and consanguinity. We must therefore acquiesce in the necessity, which denounces our Separation, and hold them, as we hold the rest of mankind, Enemies in War, in Peace Friends.

☞ Having presented its bill of indictment, the Declaration reminds its intended audience that the colonists had done everything possible to seek a peaceful resolution of their grievances, only to be rebuffed by further encroachments on their liberty. And, once again taking aim at George III, it notes that a ruler who is so deaf to the legitimate pleas of his people is nothing other than a tyrant, "unfit to be the ruler of a free people." Nor was it the king alone who had turned a deaf ear to the colonists' pleas. The Americans had warned their "British brethren" of the injustices committed upon them, but the British people as well seemed "deaf to the voice of justice and consanguinity." Reluctantly, the Americans were forced to the conclusion that "we must . . . hold them, as we hold the rest of mankind, Enemies in War, in Peace Friends." This severance of the kinship between the British subjects of the king and the people of America represented yet another step toward an irrevocable separation between mother country and colonies.

We, therefore, the Representatives of the united States of America, in General Congress, Assembled, appealing to the Supreme Judge of the world for the rectitude of our intentions, do, in the Name and by Authority of the good People of these Colonies, solemnly publish and declare, that these United Colonies are, and of Right ought to be Free and Independent States; that they are Absolved from all Allegiance to the British Crown, and that all political connection between them and the state of Great Britain is and ought to be totally dissolved; and that as Free and Independent States they have full Power to levy War, conclude Peace, contract Alliances, establish Commerce, and to do all other Acts and Things which Independent States may of right do. And for the support of this Declaration, with a firm reliance on the Protection of divine Providence, we mutually pledge to each other our Lives, our Fortunes and our sacred Honor.

GEORGIA
Button Gwinnett
Lyman Hall
George Walton

NORTH CAROLINA
William Hooper
Joseph Hewes
John Penn

SOUTH CAROLINA
Edward Rutledge
Thomas Heyward, Jr.
Thomas Lynch, Jr.
Arthur Middleton

MASSACHUSETTS
John Hancock

MARYLAND
Samuel Chase
William Paca
Thomas Stone
Charles Carroll of
  Carrollton

VIRGINIA
George Wythe
Richard Henry Lee
Thomas Jefferson
Benjamin Harrison
Thomas Nelson, Jr.
Francis Lightfoot
  Lee
Carter Braxton

PENNSYLVANIA
Robert Morris
Benjamin Rush
Benjamin Franklin
John Morton
George Clymer
James Smith
George Taylor
James Wilson
George Ross

DELAWARE
Caesar Rodney
George Read
Thomas McKean

NEW YORK
William Floyd
Philip Livingston
Francis Lewis
Lewis Morris

NEW JERSEY
Richard Stockton
John Witherspoon
Francis Hopkinson
John Hart
Abraham Clark

NEW HAMPSHIRE
Josiah Bartlett
William Whipple

MASSACHUSETTS
Samuel Adams
John Adams
Robert Treat Paine
Elbridge Gerry

RHODE ISLAND
Stephen Hopkins
William Ellery

CONNECTICUT
Roger Sherman
Samuel Huntington
William Williams
Oliver Wolcott

NEW HAMPSHIRE
Matthew Thornton

As the Declaration reaches its conclusion, it asserts for the first time that the contemplated action is one taken by the representatives of the "united States of America." And then comes the operative sentence of the Declaration of Independence: "that these United Colonies are, and of Right ought to be Free and Independent States," that they no longer have any allegiance or obligation to the British Crown or the British nation. Implicit in the final two sentences of the document is a promise whose means of fulfillment was at that moment very much unknown. The "United Colonies" were not only declaring their independence but stating their intention, as independent and *united* states, to carry out a war against one of the world's most formidable military powers, to negotiate a successful peace, to make alliances with other nations, to promote commerce, "and do all other Acts and Things which Independent States may of right do." The Americans intended not only to form independent states but also to find ways in which those independent states could unite in common cause. And to fulfill their commitment to that common cause, the Americans, in the final line of the Declaration of Independence, pledged "to each other, our Lives, our Fortunes and our sacred Honor."

THE CONSTITUTION
OF THE
UNITED STATES

We the People of the United States, in Order to form a more perfect Union, establish Justice, insure domestic Tranquility, provide for the common defence, promote the general Welfare, and secure the Blessings of Liberty to ourselves and our Posterity, do ordain and establish this Constitution for the United States of America.

☞ The preamble to the Constitution is a statement of aspiration—a promise to Americans about the things that the new federal government intended to achieve for "We the People of the United States." Some of the specific objects of government stated in the preamble— the establishment of justice, insuring the peaceful operation of society, and providing for the common defense—had long been understood to be the primary responsibilities of any government. The promises to promote the general welfare and to "secure the Blessings of Liberty" are more open-ended, suggesting that the government's responsibilities extend not merely to providing essential services but also to benevolent oversight of the polity. Although the words of the preamble do not carry the force of law, they have had substantial rhetorical power over the life of the Constitution.

ARTICLE I
SECTION I

All legislative Powers herein granted shall be vested in a Congress of the United States, which shall consist of a Senate and House of Representatives.

It is no accident that the first article of the Constitution deals with the structure and powers of the Congress, for virtually all of those who took part in the drafting of the Constitution considered the legislative branch to be the most important and, rightfully, the most powerful of the three branches of government.

There was broad agreement among the framers of the Constitution that the Congress should consist of a bicameral legislature. The House of Representatives, the "lower house," was conceived to be the "great repository" of the people of the nation at large, while the Senate, "the upper house," was to be composed of only the most knowledgeable, well-educated, and virtuous, who could be relied upon to act as a moderating influence on the whims of the people at large.

SECTION 2

The House of Representatives shall be composed of Members chosen every second Year by the People of the several States, and the Electors in each State shall have the Qualifications requisite for Electors of the most numerous Branch of the State Legislature.

No Person shall be a Representative who shall not have attained to the Age of twenty five Years, and been seven Years a Citizen of the United States, and who shall not, when elected, be an Inhabitant of that State in which he shall be chosen.

Representatives and direct Taxes shall be apportioned among the several States which may be included within this Union, according to their respective Numbers, which shall be determined by adding to the whole Number of free Persons, including those bound to Service for a Term of Years, and excluding Indians not taxed, three fifths of all other Persons. The actual Enumeration shall be made within three Years after the first Meeting of the Congress of the United States, and within every subsequent Term of ten Years, in such Manner as they shall by Law direct. The Number of Representatives shall not exceed one for every thirty Thousand, but each State shall have at Least one Representative; and until such enumeration shall be made, the State of New Hampshire shall be entitled to chuse three, Massachusetts eight, Rhode-Island and Providence Plantations one, Connecticut five, New-York six, New Jersey four, Pennsylvania eight, Delaware one, Maryland six, Virginia ten, North Carolina five, South Carolina five, and Georgia three.

When vacancies happen in the Representation from any State, the Executive Authority thereof shall issue Writs of Election to fill such Vacancies.

The House of Representatives shall chuse their Speaker and other Officers; and shall have the sole Power of Impeachment.

☞ The framers of the Constitution stipulated that members of the House of Representatives, the people's house, should serve relatively short terms of only two years, after which they would be required to seek re-election should they wish to continue to represent their state. The delegates could not agree on who should be allowed to vote for members of the House of Representatives, so they left the matter of voting requirements up to the state legislatures, which had up to that time set the qualifications for voters in each of the states. In 1787 all the states except New Jersey (which briefly permitted females to vote) limited the franchise to "free men" (a term usually interpreted to exclude free blacks) and most required that voters own at least some form of property. By the 1820s, most states had opened up the franchise to free white males regardless of whether they owned property. Subsequent amendments—the Fifteenth, prohibiting the denial of the franchise on account of "race, color, or previous condition of servitude"; the Nineteenth, enfranchising women; and the Twenty-sixth, establishing a uniform voting age of eighteen—served to create a common national standard for voting in federal elections.

The requirement that members of the House of Representatives reside in the state in which they were chosen reflected the belief that representatives, if they are to serve the people who elect them, must have close and meaningful ties to the communities in which those people live.

The "three fifths of all other Persons" referred to in this section is the result of the infamous "three-fifths compromise," in which slaves, though not mentioned by name, were to be counted as three-fifths of a person in the apportionment of representation in the House of Representatives as well as in the apportioning of the amount of direct taxes to be paid by each state. The three-fifths ratio was a purely arbitrary one. It was a consequence of a fundamental contradiction that the Convention delegates were unable to resolve: slaves were human beings, but by the laws of most states they were also regarded as property. The passage of the Thirteenth Amendment abolishing slavery rendered this portion of Article I, Section 2 null and void.

Although the original Constitution laid down a formula for representation based on population (and "three fifths of all other Persons"), none of the delegates to the 1787 Convention really knew what the actual population of each of the states was. The initial apportionment of representation was merely a guess, but the Constitution did provide for a census of the population to be taken every ten years, a practice that began in 1790 and has continued to the present day.

The "sole Power of Impeachment" referred only to the first step—the equivalent of an indictment or bringing to trial—in the removal of a federal official. The grounds for impeachment set down in Article II, Section 4—"Treason, Bribery, or other High Crimes and Misdemeanors"—have been subject to widely varying interpretations.

SECTION 3

The Senate of the United States shall be composed of two Senators from each State, chosen by the Legislature thereof, for six Years; and each Senator shall have one Vote.

Immediately after they shall be assembled in Consequence of the first Election, they shall be divided as equally as may be into three Classes. The Seats of the Senators of the first Class shall be vacated at the Expiration of the second Year, of the second Class at the Expiration of the fourth Year, and of the third Class at the Expiration of the sixth Year, so that one third may be chosen every second Year; and if Vacancies happen by Resignation, or otherwise, during the Recess of the Legislature of any State, the Executive thereof may make temporary Appointments until the next Meeting of the Legislature, which shall then fill such Vacancies.

No person shall be a Senator who shall not have attained to the Age of thirty Years, and been nine Years a Citizen of the United States, and who shall not, when elected, be an Inhabitant of that State for which he shall be chosen.

The Vice President of the United States shall be President of the Senate, but shall have no Vote, unless they be equally divided.

The Senate shall chuse their other Officers, and also a President pro tempore, in the Absence of the Vice President, or when he shall exercise the Office of President of the United States.

The Senate shall have the sole Power to try all Impeachments. When sitting for that Purpose, they shall be on Oath or Affirmation. When the President of the United States is tried, the Chief Justice shall preside: And no Person shall be convicted without the Concurrence of two thirds of the Members present.

Judgment in Cases of Impeachment shall not extend further than to removal from Office, and disqualification to hold and enjoy any Office of honor, Trust or Profit under the United States: but the Party convicted shall nevertheless be liable and subject to Indictment, Trial, Judgment and Punishment, according to Law.

☞ The Senate, as the "upper house," was conceived as a more deliberative body, whose members would be comprised of the most virtuous and knowledgeable citizens in the land. The framers of the Constitution believed that Senators should therefore serve longer terms in order that they might be better insulated from the immediate pressures of public opinion. One of the means by which Senators would be protected from popular whims was to provide for an indirect method for their election, with the legislatures of the individual states being given the power over such election. The provision for staggered terms of service was designed to prevent sudden, convulsive turnover in the membership of the Senate.

Consistent with the view that the members of the Senate were expected to possess superior knowledge and experience, the minimum age of Senators was set at thirty, and the length of time after becoming a citizen nine years, as opposed to twenty-five years of age and seven years of citizenship for members of the House of Representatives.

The framers of the Constitution were aware of the necessity of providing for a vice president, who would assume the president's duties in the event of his death, disability, or removal, but they had a hard time thinking of any other functions the vice president might perform. The provision of Article I, Section 3, designating the vice president as the presiding officer of the Senate, is the only item in the Constitution that speaks to the limited official duties of the vice president.

The Senate, as the more deliberative of the two legislative bodies, was given the responsibility of trying impeachment cases. Seeking to reinforce the principle of separation of powers, the Constitution designates the chief justice of the U.S. Supreme Court as the person who would preside over an impeachment trial of the president.

SECTION 4

The Times, Places and Manner of holding Elections for Senators and Representatives, shall be prescribed in each State by the Legislature thereof; but the Congress may at any time by Law make or alter such Regulations, except as to the Place of chusing Senators.

The Congress shall assemble at least once in every Year, and such Meeting shall be on the first Monday in December, unless they shall by Law appoint a different Day.

☞ As was the case in the instance of voting requirements, the framers of the Constitution were content to leave the matter of when congressional elections should be held to the state governments.

The stipulation that Congress should assemble on the first Monday in December was altered by the passage of the Twentieth Amendment in 1933. The practical effect of the original terms of Article I, Section 4, was to delay the seating of new members of Congress until March, creating a period of months during which a lame-duck Congress would be in session. Improvements in transportation and communications made it possible, and desirable, to move the stipulated time of the meeting of Congress to January 3.

SECTION 5

Each House shall be the Judge of the Elections, Returns and Qualifications of its own Members, and a Majority of each shall constitute a Quorum to do Business; but a smaller Number may adjourn from day to day, and may be authorized to compel the Attendance of absent Members, in such Manner, and under such Penalties as each House may provide.

Each House may determine the Rules of its Proceedings, punish its Members for disorderly Behaviour, and, with the Concurrence of two thirds, expel a Member.

Each House shall keep a Journal of its Proceedings, and from time to time publish the same, excepting such Parts as may in their Judgment require Secrecy; and the Yeas and Nays of the Members of either House on any question shall, at the Desire of one fifth of those Present, be entered on the Journal.

Neither House, during the Session of Congress, shall, without the Consent of the other, adjourn for more than three days, nor to any other Place than that in which the two Houses shall be sitting.

☞ The items in Article I, Section 5, giving each branch of the legislature control over its own proceedings, reflect a long-standing desire, dating back to the gradual evolution of the English parliament as a legislative body with powers independent of those of the king, to preserve the independence of the legislature from executive encroachment. This section of the Constitution also encourages openness in the publication and dissemination of the proceedings of Congress.

SECTION 6

The Senators and Representatives shall receive a Compensation for their Services, to be ascertained by Law, and paid out of the Treasury of the United States. They shall in all Cases, except Treason, Felony and Breach of the Peace, be privileged from Arrest during their Attendance at the Session of their respective Houses, and in going to and returning from the same; and for any Speech or Debate in either House, they shall not be questioned in any other Place.

No Senator or Representative shall, during the Time for which he was elected, be appointed to any civil Office under the Authority of the United States, which shall have been created, or the Emoluments whereof shall have been encreased during such time; and no Person holding any Office under the United States, shall be a Member of either House during his Continuance in Office.

☞ The provision for paying salaries to members of Congress provoked some disagreement among the delegates, as at least some members of the Constitutional Convention thought that public servants should be virtuous and wealthy "gentlemen" capable of serving in office without the need to seek compensation.

The provision providing immunity from arrest except in cases of treason, felony, or breach of the peace was another attempt to ensure the independence of members of the legislature, and the provision prohibiting service in other public offices while serving in Congress marked a rejection of practices in the English parliament, where members of Parliament also served as ministers in the king's cabinet; more generally it reflected a desire to reinforce the principle of separation of powers.

SECTION 7

All bills for raising Revenue shall originate in the House of Representatives; but the Senate may propose or concur with Amendments as on other Bills.

Every Bill which shall have passed the House of Representatives and the Senate, shall, before it become a Law, be presented to the President of the United States: If he approve he shall sign it, but if not he shall return it, with his Objections to that House in which it shall have originated, who shall enter the Objections at large on their Journal, and proceed to reconsider it. If after such Reconsideration two thirds of that House shall agree to pass the Bill, it shall be sent, together with the Objections, to the other House, by which it shall likewise be reconsidered, and if approved by two thirds of that House, it shall become a Law. But in all such Cases the Votes of both Houses shall be determined by Yeas and Nays, and the Names of the Persons voting for and against the Bill shall be entered on the Journal of each House respectively. If any Bill shall not be returned by the President within ten Days (Sundays excepted) after it shall have been presented to him, the Same shall be a Law, in like Manner as if he had signed it, unless the Congress by their Adjournment prevent its Return, in which Case it shall not be a Law.

Every Order, Resolution, or Vote to which the Concurrence of the Senate and House of Representatives may be necessary (except on a question of Adjournment) shall be presented to the President of the United States; and before the Same shall take Effect, shall be approved by him, or being disapproved by him, shall be repassed by two thirds of the Senate and House of Representatives, according to the Rules and Limitations prescribed in the Case of a Bill.

The power over the "purse" was considered the most important of the powers that any government could wield; indeed it was the British parliament's attempt to tax the colonies without their consent that precipitated the American Revolution. The decision to give the federal government the power to levy taxes—a power denied to the government under the Articles of Confederation—may well have been the most impor-

tant one made by the delegates to the Convention. It is
noteworthy, however, that they gave the "people's
body," the House of Representatives, the power to originate revenue bills.

The next, lengthy portion of Article I, Section 7, is
one of the hallmarks of the system of separation of
powers and checks and balances. It spells out the process by which a legislative proposal must pass both
houses of Congress and then receive the assent of the
president before it can become law. It provides for a
limited executive veto over congressional legislation
but gives to the Congress the power, if it can muster a
two-thirds majority, to override a presidential veto.

SECTION 8

The Congress shall have Power To lay and collect
Taxes, Duties, Imposts and Excises, to pay the Debts
and provide for the common Defence and general
Welfare of the United States; but all Duties, Imposts
and Excises shall be uniform throughout the United
States:

To Borrow Money on the credit of the United
States;

To regulate Commerce with foreign Nations, and
among the several States, and with the Indian Tribes;

To establish an uniform Rule of Naturalization,
and uniform Laws on the subject of Bankruptcies
throughout the United States;

To coin Money, regulate the Value thereof, and of

foreign Coin, and fix the Standard of Weights and Measures;

To provide for the Punishment of counterfeiting the Securities and current Coin of the United States;

To establish Post Offices and Post Roads;

To promote the Progress of Science and useful Arts, by securing for limited Times to Authors and Inventors the exclusive Right to their respective Writings and Discoveries;

To constitute Tribunals inferior to the supreme Court;

To define and punish Piracies and Felonies committed on the high Seas, and Offences against the Law of Nations;

To declare War, grant Letters of Marque and Reprisal, and make Rules concerning Captures on Land and Water;

To raise and support Armies, but no Appropriation of Money to that Use shall be for a longer Term than two Years;

To provide and maintain a Navy;

To make Rules for the Government and Regulation of the land and naval Forces;

To provide for calling forth the Militia to execute the Laws of the Union, suppress Insurrections and repel Invasions;

To provide for organizing, arming, and disciplining the Militia, and for governing such Part of them as may be employed in the Service of the United States, reserving to the States respectively, the Appointment of the Officers, and the Authority of training the Militia according to the discipline prescribed by Congress;

To exercise exclusive Legislation in all Cases whatsoever, over such District (not exceeding ten Miles square) as may, by Cession of particular States, and the Acceptance of Congress, become the Seat of the Government of the United States, and to exercise like Authority over all Places purchased by the Consent of the Legislature of the State in which the Same shall be, for the Erection of Forts, Magazines, Arsenals, dock-Yards, and other needful Buildings;—And

To make all Laws which shall be necessary and proper for carrying into Execution the foregoing Powers, and all other Powers vested by this Constitution in the Government of the United States, or in any Department or Officer thereof.

☞ Many Americans think of their Constitution as a document that protects the liberties of American citizens by defining those things that the federal government *cannot* do. This is the central concern of the first ten amendments to the Constitution, which today we call the Bill of Rights. But in fact, in many respects Article I, Section 8, constitutes the heart and soul of the U.S. Constitution. It specifically enumerates the powers that the federal government is permitted to exercise. The initial version of this article, as outlined in the Virginia Plan, gave an open-ended grant of power to the Congress, simply providing that Congress would have the power "to legislate in all cases to which the separate States are incompetent," but when the Committee of Detail produced a comprehensive first draft of a constitution in early August 1787, that general grant of power was replaced by the more specific enumeration of powers that appears in Article I, Section 8. Among the most important powers enumerated in Article I, Section 8, are:

1. As previously mentioned, the power to levy taxes— the ability of the government to provide for itself a permanent revenue with which to finance its operations—was the single most important power given to the new federal government. The broad purposes for which that power was granted—to "provide for the common Defence and general Welfare of the United States"—have been interpreted in widely different ways over the course of the nation's history, with the general trend leading toward an expansion of activity financed by the federal taxation power.

2. The "commerce power" has proven to be one of the most important and far-reaching provisions of the federal Constitution. Utilizing an ever-expanding definition of its power to regulate commerce "among the several States," the federal government has broadened the definition of "commerce" to include not only the shipment of goods across state lines but also many other forms of activity: the building of interstate roads; the power to regulate the

business activities of corporations; and the power to pass environmental legislation, consumer-protection laws, and occupational-safety regulations.

3. Establishing post offices and post roads may seem mundane enterprises, but this provision of the Constitution, in conjunction with an expansive view of Congress's role in promoting the "general Welfare" and regulating commerce, marked the beginnings of the creation of a national infrastructure that would tie the thirteen previously independent and sovereign states into a single nation.

4. The clause relating to the promotion of science and useful arts gives to Congress the power to enact patent and copyright laws.

5. Clauses ten through sixteen of Article I, Section 8, deal with the war powers of Congress. If the "power over the purse" has long been considered to be the most important of a government's powers, the power over the "sword"—the ability not only to declare war but also to vote on appropriations for the financial support of war—has run a close second. Congress's power to declare war overlaps with the power of the president, as commander in chief of the nation's armed forces, to direct the actual conduct of war. In one sense, this overlap is part of the Constitution's system of separation of powers, but in another it has become a significant source of constitutional controversy in recent years. In numerous cases since the mid-twentieth century—

in the Korean War, the Vietnam War, the First Gulf War, and most recently, the wars in Iraq and Afghanistan—the president has proceeded with the prosecution of the war without a formal congressional declaration of war.

6. Congress's power over the appropriation of money gives it a substantial say over how—or whether—a war should be fought, but it has only rarely denied funds for the support of an army or navy once a war is under way.

7. The seventeenth clause, giving to Congress the power to "exercise exclusive Legislation . . . over such District . . . as may . . . become the Seat of the Government," is the basis on which Congress created the District of Columbia, which is regarded not as a state but as a federal territory and the nation's capital.

8. The final provision of Article I, Section 8, has proven to be one of the most important—and controversial—provisions of the Constitution. By giving Congress the power to make all laws "necessary and proper" for carrying into effect the previously enumerated powers, the framers of the Constitution opened the door to a significant expansion of federal power. Within just a few years of the adoption of the Constitution, some of the most important figures of the revolutionary era found themselves in bitter disagreement on the meaning of the phrase "necessary and proper," with President Washington's secretary of the treasury, Alex-

ander Hamilton, arguing for a broad construction of its meaning (for example, as "needful," "useful," or "conducive to") and Thomas Jefferson and James Madison arguing for a strict construction (for example, as "absolutely necessary"). This line of constitutional difference between "broad constructionists" and "strict constructionists" was a bitter source of contention in the period leading up to the Civil War and continues in somewhat diminished form between the respective proponents of a more limited or more active federal government even today.

SECTION 9

The Migration or Importation of such Persons as any of the States now existing shall think proper to admit, shall not be prohibited by the Congress prior to the Year one thousand eight hundred and eight, but a Tax or duty may be imposed on such Importation, not exceeding ten dollars for each Person.

The Privilege of the Writ of Habeas Corpus shall not be suspended, unless when in Cases of Rebellion or Invasion the public Safety may require it.

No Bill of Attainder or ex post facto Law shall be passed.

No Capitation, or other direct, Tax shall be laid, unless in Proportion to the Census or Enumeration herein before directed to be taken.

No Tax or Duty shall be laid on Articles exported from any State.

No Preference shall be given by any Regulation of Commerce or Revenue to the Ports of one State over those of another; nor shall Vessels bound to, or from, one State, be obliged to enter, clear, or pay Duties in another.

No Money shall be drawn from the Treasury, but in Consequence of Appropriations made by Law; and a regular Statement and Account of the Receipts and Expenditures of all public Money shall be published from time to time.

No Title of Nobility shall be granted by the United States: And no Person holding any Office of Profit or Trust under them, shall, without the Consent of the Congress, accept of any present, Emolument, Office, or Title, of any kind whatever, from any King, Prince or foreign State.

☞ Article I, Section 9, outlines those actions that the federal government *may not* take.

The most controversial of these prohibitions is contained in the very first item. The Convention delegates from South Carolina and Georgia, whose slave economies were still expanding, insisted that no legislation interfering with the African slave trade be permitted until at least twenty years after the adoption of the Constitution. The prohibition of any legislation affecting "the Migration or Importation of such Persons as any of the States now existing shall think proper to admit" was intended to ensure that protection. As in all instances in which the Constitution deals with the institution of slavery, neither the word "slave" nor "slavery" is explicitly mentioned in the text of the document. In 1808 the U.S. Congress enacted legislation abolishing the international slave trade, but during that twenty-year interval some two hundred thousand slaves were imported from Africa into the United States.

Many of the most important prohibitions to federal government action laid down in Article I, Section 9, were designed to protect fundamental liberties handed down to Americans through English common law. Perhaps the most important of these was the privilege of habeas corpus, the right of a prisoner to challenge his imprisonment in a court of law. On at least a few occasions American presidents have suspended this privilege while either suppressing rebellion or protecting the public safety. During the Civil War, President Abraham Lincoln held "disloyal persons" suspected of giving aid and comfort to the Confederate cause in prison without benefit of trial. More recently, President George W. Bush, citing provisions of the Patriot Act as well as implied executive powers, sanctioned the holding of several hundred "enemy combatants" in the "war on terror."

The prohibition against bills of attainder, the issuing of edicts aimed at punishing individuals or groups of individuals without benefit of trial, and the ban on ex post facto laws—criminal laws aimed at punishing individuals for actions taken before the law itself was passed—were also rooted in traditions of English common law. The prohibition of taxes on exports was a purely political bargain between northern and southern states, and was designed to protect the interests of the South, whose agricultural exports formed an important part of its economy. The prohibition against direct taxes unless such taxes were levied precisely in proportion to the number of citizens in each of the states was another attempt to protect the institution of slavery from being taxed out of existence; this provision was subsequently changed by the passage of the Sixteenth Amendment, making possible the imposition of a federal income tax.

While it would be unthinkable today for our federal government to grant a title of nobility to any of its citizens, the provision in Article I, Section 9, prohibiting the granting of titles of nobility and placing additional restrictions on receiving a "present, Emolument, Office, or Title" from a foreign state reflected the strong commitment of the framers of the Constitution that their government should be a "republican" one, and not one that reflected the aristocratic ways of Europe.

SECTION 10

No State shall enter into any Treaty, Alliance, or Confederation; grant Letters of Marque and Reprisal; coin Money; emit Bills of Credit; make any Thing but gold and silver Coin a Tender in Payment of Debts; pass any Bill of Attainder, ex post facto Law, or Law impairing the Obligation of Contracts, or grant any Title of Nobility.

No State shall, without the Consent of the Congress, lay any Imposts or Duties on Imports or Exports, except what may be absolutely necessary for executing its inspection Laws: and the net Produce of all Duties and Imposts, laid by any State on Imports or Exports, shall be for the Use of the Treasury of the United States; and all such Laws shall be subject to the Revision and Controul of the Congress.

No State shall, without the Consent of Congress, lay any duty of Tonnage, keep Troops, or Ships of War in time of Peace, enter into any Agreement or Compact with another State, or with a foreign Power, or engage in War, unless actually invaded, or in such imminent Danger as will not admit of delay.

☞ The provisions in Article I, Section 10, stipulate those things that the *state governments* are prohibited from doing. The most important of these are:

1. Individual states may not enter into separate treaties with foreign nations.
2. The governments of the states are bound by the same requirements as the federal government in the prohibition of bills of attainder, ex post facto laws, laws impairing obligations of contracts, and granting titles of nobility.
3. State governments may not issue currency for the

purpose of paying debts unless that currency is in gold and silver. This provision came in reaction to the laxness of some state governments that issued depreciated or, in some cases, worthless currency during the period of the Revolution. This provision marked the beginning—but only the beginning—of the creation of a single national currency.

4. During the period of the Confederation, many states, eager to raise their own revenues, levied tariffs on goods entering their ports from other states. The new Constitution reserved the power of taxing imports to the federal government alone, preventing states from enacting their own tariffs.

5. Although the individual states were permitted to maintain their own militias for the maintenance of order within their boundaries, the Constitution prohibits states from maintaining either a standing army or a navy in time of peace; it also prohibits the states from entering into agreements with other states or foreign powers for military purposes.

ARTICLE II
SECTION I

The executive Power shall be vested in a President of the United States of America. He shall hold his Office during the Term of four Years, and, together with the Vice President, chosen for the same Term, be elected, as follows:

Each State shall appoint, in such Manner as the Legislature thereof may direct, a Number of Electors, equal to the whole Number of Senators and Representatives to which the State may be entitled in the Congress: but no Senator or Representative, or Person holding an Office of Trust or Profit under the United States, shall be appointed an Elector.

The Electors shall meet in their respective States, and vote by Ballot for two Persons, of whom one at least shall not be an Inhabitant of the same State with themselves. And they shall make a List of all the Persons voted for, and of the Number of Votes for each; which List they shall sign and certify, and transmit sealed to the Seat of the Government of the United States, directed to the President of the Senate. The President of the Senate shall, in the Presence of the Senate and House of Representatives, open all the Certificates, and the Votes shall then be counted. The Person having the greatest Number of Votes shall be the President, if such Number be a Majority of the whole Number of Electors appointed; and if there be more than one who have such Majority, and have an equal Number of Votes, then the House of Representatives shall immediately chuse by Ballot one of them for President; and if no Person have a Majority, then from the five highest on the List the said House shall in like Manner chuse the President. But in chusing the President, the Votes shall be taken by States, the Representation from each State having one Vote; a quorum for this Purpose shall consist of a Member or Members from two thirds of the States, and a Majority of all the States shall be necessary to a Choice. In every Case, after the Choice of the President, the Person having the greatest Number of Votes of the Electors shall be the Vice President. But if there should remain two or more who have equal Votes, the Senate shall chuse from them by Ballot the Vice President.

The Congress may determine the Time of chusing the Electors, and the Day on which they shall give their Votes; which Day shall be the same throughout the United States.

No person except a natural born Citizen, or a Citizen of the United States, at the time of the Adoption of this Constitution, shall be eligible to the Office of President; neither shall any Person be eligible to that Office who shall not have attained to the Age of thirty five Years, and been fourteen Years a Resident within the United States.

In Case of the Removal of the President from Office, or of his Death, Resignation, or Inability to discharge the Powers and Duties of the said Office, the Same shall devolve on the Vice President, and the Congress may by Law provide for the Case of Removal, Death, Resignation or Inability, both of the President and Vice President, declaring what Officer shall then act as President, and such Officer shall act accordingly, until the Disability be removed, or a President shall be elected.

The President shall, at stated Times, receive for his

Services, a Compensation, which shall neither be increased nor diminished during the Period for which he shall have been elected, and he shall not receive within that Period any other Emolument from the United States, or any of them.

Before he enter on the Execution of his Office, he shall take the following Oath or Affirmation: "I do solemnly swear (or affirm) that I will faithfully execute the Office of President of the United States, and will to the best of my Ability, preserve, protect and defend the Constitution of the United States."

☞ The opening words of Article II, Section 1, are both remarkably simple and maddeningly vague: "The executive Power shall be vested in a President of the United States of America." While other sections of Article II provide some specificity on the nature and extent of presidential power, for the most part the language of Article II relating to executive power is far less specific than that of Article I defining congressional power.

Opinions about the length of the president's term varied widely, with proposals ranging from a minimum of two years to a term of "during good behavior"—or, effectively, for life. The delegates also disagreed about whether the president should be eligible for reelection. The decision on a four-year term seemed to satisfy most delegates and, by avoiding mentioning anything about the president's eligibility for reelection, the framers left the question of how many terms a president should serve up to the voters. George Washington's decision to serve only two terms in office set a precedent that lasted until the presidency of Franklin D. Roosevelt, who won election to the presidency four times, serving from 1933 until his death in 1945. In 1951 Congress passed, and the states ratified, the Twenty-second Amendment, limiting presidents to two terms.

The next part of Article II, Section 1, reflects the torment the Convention delegates experienced as they wrestled with the question of how to give the president sufficient power without giving him excessive power, as well as how to free him from excessive dependence on the legislature while at the same time assuring that he did not become, in their terms, an "elective monarch." While one would think that the best way to do this would be to have the president elected by and answerable to the people of the nation at large, the vast majority of delegates feared that the American people were simply too provincial—too ignorant of the merits of possible presidential candidates across a land as vast as that of the thirteen states of which America was then comprised—to make a wise choice. For that reason, for most of the Convention the delegates inclined toward election of the president by the Congress or, at least, by the more popular branch of Congress, the House of Representatives. But this method ran the risk of violating the principles of separation of powers by making the president unduly dependent upon the Congress for his election. For much of the summer of 1787, the delegates argued unproductively about various alternatives for electing the president, and finally, in the tortured language of Article II, Section 1, they called for the creation of an electoral college: a group of independent electors, selected in each of the states "in such Manner as the Legislature thereof may direct," who would then cast their ballots for a president and vice president.

Although initially designed as a decidedly elitist device by which only the most knowledgeable and distinguished men—those selected to be electors—would use their own independent judgment in casting their ballots for the president, by the election of Thomas Jefferson in 1800 the presidential electoral system had been entirely transformed by the unexpected invention of organized political parties. The newly created political party system functioned in a way that caused slates of presidential electors to be pledged in advance to vote for particular candidates, with the result being that American voters, whose num-bers were expanding as the number of citizens eligible to vote expanded, were now casting their votes, not on the basis of the identity of the individual electors, but on the merits of the candidates themselves. The invention of political parties—a development occurring wholly outside America's constitutional system—fundamentally changed the way the Constitution operated, transforming it from a "republican" but elitist political system into a truly democratic one.

Americans have grumbled about the imperfections of the electoral college system from the days when it was first debated in the Constitutional Convention up to the present, but for the most part, it has managed to produce victors in the presidential contests whose legitimacy as duly elected chief executives has not been challenged. There have been exceptions: the election of John Quincy Adams, decided by the House of Representatives in 1824; the election of a "minority" Republican president, Abraham Lincoln, in 1860, which led to the secession of the Southern states; the disputed 1876 presidential election between Samuel Tilden and Rutherford B. Hayes, in the final days of Reconstruction; and the contested election of George W. Bush in 2000, ultimately decided by the Supreme Court. Each of these cases has provoked criticism of the electoral college system, but up to this point neither Congress nor the American people have moved to the obvious alternative: direct popular election of the president.

The decision to require that the president be a "natural born Citizen" of the United States was made in the Convention with little discussion and probably with little thought. Indeed, eight of the delegates to the Convention had themselves been born outside British North America (all were born in the British Isles and would in any case have been eligible to serve as president because they were citizens of the United States at the time of the adoption of the Constitution). In an age in which America's economy, culture, and politics are increasingly shaped by recent immigrants, this particular constitutional provision seems a good candidate for amendment.

This provision defines the vice president's most important duty: to succeed the president in case of his death, disability, or removal from office. The framers left the line of succession in the event of the vice president's death, disability, resignation, or removal up to Congress. The Twenty-fifth Amendment, adopted in 1967, provided a means by which a president could select, with the confirmation of a majority of members of Congress, another vice president.

Although Congress is given responsibility for setting the president's salary, it may not increase or decrease his salary during his term of service, a provision designed to render the president independent of the Congress's will.

The presidential oath is a remarkably simple one, wholly appropriate to a republican society. It has often been asserted that George Washington, when he took his oath of office on April 30, 1789, added the words "So help me God" to his oath; there is, however, no written evidence to prove this assertion. We do know that from the time Abraham Lincoln took the oath of office for his second presidential term in 1865, a significant number of presidents—perhaps a majority of them—have added that phrase in taking their oath of office.

SECTION 2

The President shall be Commander in Chief of the Army and Navy of the United States, and of the Militia of the several States, when called into the actual Service of the United States; he may require the Opinion, in writing, of the principal Officer in each of the executive Departments, upon any Subject relating to the Duties of their respective Offices, and he shall have Power to grant Reprieves and Pardons for Offences against the United States, except in Cases of Impeachment.

He shall have Power, by and with the Advice and Consent of the Senate, to make Treaties, provided two thirds of the Senators present concur; and he shall nominate, and by and with the Advice and Consent of the Senate, shall appoint Ambassadors, other public Ministers and Consuls, Judges of the supreme Court, and all other Officers of the United States, whose Appointments are not herein otherwise provided for, and which shall be established by Law: but the Congress may by Law vest the Appointment of such inferior Officers, as they think proper, in the President alone, in the Courts of Law, or in the Heads of Departments.

The President shall have Power to fill up all Vacancies that may happen during the Recess of the Senate, by granting Commissions which shall expire at the End of their next Session.

Article II, Section 2, is principally concerned with outlining the powers of the president, but given the enormous power of the modern presidency, it seems remarkably short and vague in its prescriptions. Certainly, the most important—and controversial—of those powers has devolved from the president's role as commander in chief of the army and navy of the United States and of the militias of the several states. That role, which has given the president enormous power to "make war," has sometimes come in conflict with the power of Congress to "declare war" as well as with Congress's power to control the financial appropriations necessary to make fighting a war possible.

By the terms of Article II, Section 2, the president has the primary role in entering into treaties with other nations, although it reserves to the Senate the right to approve any treaty before it assumes the force of law.

The president has the power, with the advice and consent of the Senate, to appoint ambassadors, ministers, justices of the Supreme Court, and "all other Officers of the United States." In recent decades, as the Supreme Court has become a more powerful and assertive branch of the federal government, members of the Senate have responded by asserting more vigorously *their* right to advise and consent with respect to the appointment of justices of the Court.

The president's use of the power to appoint "all other Officers of the United States" has increased in direct proportion to the growing power of the federal government and of the executive branch in particular. Although the Founding Fathers no doubt assumed that the president would appoint members of a presidential "cabinet," they would perhaps have been surprised at the growth in the size and scope of the bureaucracy serving each of the cabinet departments. The president's cabinet has expanded from four members in President Washington's day (the secretaries of treasury, war, and state and the attorney general) to fifteen (not including the vice president) today.

SECTION 3

He shall from time to time give to the Congress Information of the State of the Union, and recommend to their Consideration such Measures as he shall judge necessary and expedient; he may, on extraordinary Occasions, convene both Houses, or either of them, and in Case of Disagreement between them, with Respect to the Time of Adjournment, he may adjourn them to such Time as he shall think proper; he shall receive Ambassadors and other public Ministers; he shall take Care that the Laws be faithfully executed, and shall Commission all the Officers of the United States.

☞ Presidents Washington and Adams addressed the Congress directly on the "State of the Union," but from 1801 to 1909 the president merely sent the Congress written messages. Beginning in 1913, and continuing to the present day, the formal State of the Union address to Congress, given at the beginning of each year, has become an important national ritual. Some presidents, including President Barack Obama, have convened both houses of Congress on other "extraordinary Occasions," to address them on subjects that they have considered important.

SECTION 4

The President, Vice President and all civil Officers of the United States, shall be removed from Office on Impeachment for, and Conviction of, Treason, Bribery, or other high Crimes and Misdemeanors.

☞ This is another one of the provisions of Article II that is remarkably simple and maddeningly vague. The framers of the Constitution all agreed that a president should be removed from office if he committed treason, bribery, or other "high Crimes," but most of them also believed that the president might be removed if he were found culpable of "malfeasance in office" (a term used in one of the earlier drafts of the Constitution). On the other hand, most of the framers agreed that it would be improper for Congress to remove a president simply because a majority of members of Congress might disagree with him, and since "malfeasance" was a term with a meaning that might vary in the eye of the beholder, they substituted the term "Misdemeanors" for "malfeasance." It was a term that left no one wholly satisfied, and it has caused considerable confusion in those rare cases (during the presidencies of Andrew Johnson, Richard Nixon, and William Jefferson Clinton) in which impeachment proceedings against a president have been initiated.

ARTICLE III
SECTION 1

The judicial Power of the United States shall be vested in one supreme Court, and in such inferior Courts as the Congress may from time to time ordain and establish. The Judges, both of the supreme and inferior Courts, shall hold their Offices during good Behaviour, and shall, at stated Times, receive for their Services a Compensation which shall not be diminished during their Continuance in Office.

☞ Just as the framers of the Constitution considered the Congress to be the most vital branch of the new government and therefore dealt with that branch in the very first article of the Constitution, so too was the placement of the judicial branch in Article III of the Constitution a reflection of their view of the relative importance of that branch. The brevity and vagueness of the language in Article III are similarly a reflection of their relative lack of concern about the judicial branch as well as of their uncertainty about its function in the new federal union.

Article III, Section 1, stipulates that there would be one "supreme" court in the nation but is vague about the number and extent of the "inferior" courts. The provision that all federal judges should hold their offices during "good Behaviour" was intended to protect the independence of the judiciary and reinforce the separation of powers among the three branches of the new government.

SECTION 2

The judicial Power shall extend to all Cases, in Law and Equity, arising under this Constitution, the Laws of the United States, and Treaties made, or which shall be made, under their Authority; to all Cases affecting Ambassadors, other public Ministers and Consuls; to all Cases of admiralty and maritime Jurisdiction; to Controversies to which the United States shall be a Party; to Controversies between two or more States; between a State and Citizens of another State; between Citizens of different States; between Citizens of the same State claiming Lands under Grants of different States; and between a State, or the Citizens thereof, and foreign States, Citizens or Subjects.

In all Cases affecting Ambassadors, other public Ministers and Consuls, and those in which a State shall be Party, the supreme Court shall have original Jurisdiction. In all the other Cases before mentioned, the supreme Court shall have appellate Jurisdiction, both as to Law and Fact, with such Exceptions, and under such Regulations as the Congress shall make.

The Trial of all Crimes, except in Cases of Impeachment, shall be by Jury; and such Trial shall be held in the State where the said Crimes shall have been committed; but when not committed within any

State, the Trial shall be at such Place or Places as the Congress may by Law have directed.

🖝 Article III, Section 2, defines the jurisdiction and mode of procedure of the federal courts. The key phrase is "to all Cases, in Law and Equity, arising under this Constitution." In other words, the jurisdiction of the federal courts extends to those areas in which the United States government itself has jurisdiction. That jurisdiction, vaguely defined in 1787, has steadily increased over the more than two centuries in which the Constitution has been in operation.

Although Article III, Section 2, makes no mention of a power of judicial review (the power of the Supreme Court or any other federal court to pass judgment on whether a federal or state law violates the terms of the Constitution), many, if not most, of the delegates to the Convention probably assumed that the federal courts would exercise at least some limited form of that power. In 1803, in the case of *Marbury v. Madison*, the Supreme Court, in an opinion written by its chief justice, John Marshall, enunciated a limited power of judicial review.

SECTION 3

Treason against the United States, shall consist only in levying War against them, or in adhering to their Enemies, giving them Aid and Comfort. No Person shall be convicted of Treason unless on the Testimony of two Witnesses to the same overt Act, or on Confession in open Court.

The Congress shall have power to declare the Punishment of Treason, but no Attainder of Treason shall work Corruption of Blood, or Forfeiture except during the Life of the Person attainted.

☞ Article III, Section 3, is the only instance in which the U.S. Constitution defines a specific crime, that of treason. Treason is defined either as levying war against the United States or as giving "Aid and Comfort" to the enemies of the United States. The "Aid and Comfort" clause expands the definition of treason beyond physical acts of violence—e.g., to the passing on of state secrets to another nation—but the Constitution also lays down specific legal procedures by which people accused of treason might be convicted of such an act. The Constitution further limits the punishment of treason to the person actually committing the act, not to family members or close associates.

In 1807, in the treason trial of Aaron Burr, for his role in an alleged plan to lead parts of the Louisiana territory in a secessionist movement from the United States, Chief Justice John Marshall laid down further limitations on the definition of treason, establishing the doctrine of "constructive treason," meaning that the mere planning of an act that might be considered treasonous was not sufficient grounds for conviction; in order to be convicted of treason one actually had to commit, or at least be in the process of committing, the act. Moreover, the act of simply speaking, however stridently, in a manner that some might believe to be giving aid and comfort to the enemy was given further protection by the free speech guarantees of the First Amendment.

ARTICLE IV
SECTION I

Full Faith and Credit shall be given in each State to the public Acts, Records, and judicial Proceedings of every other State. And the Congress may by general Laws prescribe the Manner in which such Acts, Records and Proceedings shall be proved, and the Effect thereof.

The first section of Article IV stipulates that the laws of one state must be given "full Faith and Credit" (i.e., be recognized as legitimate) in another state. This provision was an important step in creating a uniform standard of law and of rights in the nation. For example, if the state of Massachusetts recognizes the marriage of a gay couple as legally valid, then other states, even if they do not have laws permitting the marriage of a gay couple, must recognize that marriage as valid.

SECTION 2

The Citizens of each State shall be entitled to all Privileges and Immunities of Citizens in the several States.

A Person charged in any State with Treason, Felony, or other Crime, who shall flee from Justice, and be found in another State, shall on Demand of the executive Authority of the State from which he fled, be delivered up, to be removed to the State having Jurisdiction of the Crime.

No Person held to Service or Labour in one State, under the Laws thereof, escaping into another, shall, in Consequence of any Law or Regulation therein, be discharged from such Service or Labour, but shall be delivered up on Claim of the Party to whom such Service or Labour may be due.

🖎 The first provision of Article IV, Section 2, is a cornerstone of a common standard for equal protection under the law for all American citizens. It gives to citizens of every state all the legal protections enjoyed by citizens of other states if they should be residing in or traveling through one of those other states. This means, for example, that New Jersey cannot give citizens of that state one set of rights while at the same time denying a citizen of New York living or working in New Jersey any of those same rights. Therefore New Jersey cannot impose higher taxes on New Yorkers working in New Jersey than it imposes on its own residents.

The other side of the "privileges and immunity" clause is that which requires states to respect the laws of other states aimed at punishing persons charged with "Treason, Felony, or other Crime" by extraditing (delivering up) such persons to the state having jurisdiction over the crime.

The final part of Article IV, Section 2, may well be the most reprehensible provision in the original U.S. Constitution. It requires that the governments and citizens of every state in the union deliver up all persons "held to Service or Labour in one State, under the Laws thereof, escaping into another." Although nowhere mentioned, those persons "held to Service or Labour" were slaves, and by requiring that citizens and states where slavery was not permitted cooperate with citizens and governments in slave-owning states in the return of their slaves, it made all Americans actively complicit in protecting the institution of slavery. This provision was rendered null and void by the passage of the Thirteenth Amendment, which abolished slavery.

SECTION 3

New States may be admitted by the Congress into this Union; but no new State shall be formed or erected within the Jurisdiction of any other State; nor any State be formed by the Junction of two or more

States, or Parts of States, without the Consent of the Legislatures of the States concerned as well as of the Congress.

The Congress shall have Power to dispose of and make all needful Rules and Regulations respecting the Territory or other Property belonging to the United States; and nothing in this Constitution shall be so construed as to Prejudice any Claims of the United States, or of any particular State.

In 1787 the framers of the Constitution were mindful that, in addition to the thirteen original states, America consisted of a vast territory between the borders of those states and the Mississippi River. Article IV, Section 3, grants to Congress the authority to admit new states into the union on an equal basis with existing states. However, individual states are not permitted either to divide themselves into separate states (for example, California, by the terms of the Constitution, is not permitted to divide itself into two states; e.g., Northern California and Southern California), nor is it possible for two or more states (for example, Rhode Island and Connecticut) to combine their territories into a single state without the consent both of the legislatures of the states involved and of Congress.

The second part of Article IV, Section 3, gives to Congress considerable leeway as to what it might do in territories that have not achieved the status of a state within the federal union. Under this provision, Congress was able to grant independence to the Philippines, which was once a territory of the United States, and to extend certain rights (for example, the right of U.S. citizenship, although not the right to vote in presidential elections) to territories like Puerto Rico. This congressional jurisdiction also extends to the District of Columbia, which, though its citizens enjoy most of the rights of citizens of the fifty American states, is not at present fully represented in Congress.

SECTION 4

The United States shall guarantee to every State in this Union a Republican Form of Government, and shall protect each of them against Invasion; and on Application of the Legislature, or of the Executive (when the Legislature cannot be convened), against domestic Violence.

☞ If there is a single idea expressed in Section 4 of Article IV on which all the framers of the Constitution agreed, it was that America should have a republican form of government, both in the polities of the individual states and in the new federal structure that they were creating. However, there were probably as many variations in the meaning of the word "republican" as there were delegates, ranging from those who wanted a democratic government directly responsive to the people to those who wished for a more elitist government, responsible to—but somewhat removed from—the people at large. The two core elements of republicanism on which all delegates could agree were that the government should be, either directly or indirectly, "representative" in character and that its officeholders should not base their claims to public office on hereditary privilege.

The second item in this section of Article IV was a direct response to one of the events that precipitated the calling of a Constitutional Convention: an armed uprising of farmers in western Massachusetts, known as Shays' Rebellion. The Constitution promises states protection against both internal uprisings and invasions from abroad but at the same time assures the states that the government will not interfere in their defense unless asked to do so by officials in the states themselves.

ARTICLE V

The Congress, whenever two thirds of both Houses shall deem it necessary, shall propose Amendments to this Constitution, or, on the Application of the Legislatures of two thirds of the several States, shall call a Convention for proposing Amendments, which, in either Case, shall be valid to all Intents and Purposes, as Part of this Constitution, when ratified by the Legislatures of three fourths of the several States, or by Conventions in three fourths thereof, as the one or the other Mode of Ratification may be proposed by the Congress; Provided that no Amendment which may be made prior to the Year one thousand eight hundred and eight shall in any Manner affect the first and fourth Clauses in the Ninth Section of the first Article; and that no State, without its Consent, shall be deprived of its equal Suffrage in the Senate.

The Constitutional Convention of 1787 was called together to amend the Articles of Confederation, the existing frame of government that sought to create a union among the thirteen independent and sovereign states. By the terms of the Articles of Confederation, unanimous approval of all of the state legislatures was required to amend any major feature of that frame of government. That provision proved to be fatally flawed, for it soon became apparent that it was impossible to attain unanimity on any matter of consequence. The delegates to the Constitutional Convention, having already gone forward not merely with amendments to the Articles of Confederation but rather with a decision to scrap the Articles altogether and create a vastly strengthened central government, felt no compunctions about changing the formula for amendment, providing two different routes by which the new Constitution could be amended. Amendments can be proposed either by a two-thirds vote of both houses of Congress or when two-thirds of the legislatures of the states agree on calling a national convention for the purpose of proposing amendments. Amendments proposed by either method must, in order to become part of the Constitution, receive the approval of three-quarters of the state legislatures or be approved by specially called conventions in at least three-quarters of the states. Most of the amendments to the Constitution have been first proposed by Congress and then adopted by three-quarters of the state legislatures, although the Twenty-first Amendment, repealing prohibition, was adopted by conventions in three-quarters of the states.

The amendment process is an arduous one, and for that reason, relatively few amendments have been passed during the more than two hundred years since the Constitution was adopted, making it one of the most concise written constitutions in the world. Ten of the amendments—those that we consider to be part of the Bill of Rights—were proposed by the First Congress of the United States and quickly adopted by the necessary number of states within a few years after the new government commenced operation. During the whole of the nineteenth century, only five amendments were adopted, three of them coming in the immediate aftermath of the Civil War and dealing with the rights of newly freed slaves. Twelve amendments were passed in the twentieth century. Among the most important were those authorizing a federal income tax, giving women a constitutional right to vote, providing for direct election of United States Senators, and guaranteeing all American citizens eighteen years or older the right to vote.

Article V also mentions three specific instances in

which the Constitution is not subject to amendment: the provision prohibiting legislation affecting the international slave trade until 1808, the prohibition against direct taxation unless apportioned according to population, and the provision guaranteeing each state equal representation in the United States Senate.

ARTICLE VI

All Debts contracted and Engagements entered into, before the Adoption of this Constitution, shall be as valid against the United States under this Constitution, as under the Confederation.

This Constitution, and the Laws of the United States which shall be made in Pursuance thereof; and all Treaties made, or which shall be made, under the Authority of the United States, shall be the supreme Law of the Land; and the Judges in every State shall be bound thereby, any Thing in the Constitution or Laws of any State to the Contrary notwithstanding.

The Senators and Representatives before mentioned, and the Members of the several State Legislatures, and all executive and judicial Officers, both of the United States and of the several States, shall be bound by Oath or Affirmation, to support this Constitution; but no religious Test shall ever be required as a Qualification to any Office or public Trust under the United States.

☞ At the time the Constitution was created, the Continental government, the individual governments of the states, and many private citizens had all accumulated substantial debt obligations. The first item in Article VI was designed to ensure the sanctity of those debt obligations.

Article VI contains the so-called federal supremacy clause, the assertion that in cases of conflict between a state law and a federal law, the federal law takes precedence. Over the course of the nation's history, there have been hundreds of cases where the overlapping jurisdictions of the states and the federal government (for example, in matters relating to the regulation of commerce, industry, or environmental policy) have led to lawsuits. In general, although not uniformly, the federal supremacy clause has worked to incline courts to side with the federal government.

The final item in Article VI requires officials in both the state and federal governments to uphold the Constitution of the United States. This item is also the only place in the body of the Constitution where religion is explicitly mentioned. It is notable that this sole mention of religion reinforces the principle of separation of church and state, decreeing that there shall be no religious test for holding public office.

ARTICLE VII

The Ratification of the Conventions of nine States, shall be sufficient for the Establishment of this Constitution between the States so ratifying the Same.

☞ Having exceeded their instructions from the Continental Congress by scrapping the Articles of Confederation and drafting a wholly new frame of government, the framers of the Constitution also ignored the provision in the Articles of Confederation requiring unanimous approval of the state legislatures in order to amend that frame of government. The decision to allow the Constitution to go into operation after the approval of only nine of the thirteen states made it much easier to secure ratification of the document. Moreover, the device of submitting the document for consideration by specially called state conventions rather than by state legislatures avoided some of the natural tendencies of state legislators to protect their powers and interests. Most important though, the use of conventions, elected directly by the people of the states and called together solely for the purpose of considering the new plan of union, signified that the proposed new government was intended to be a government founded on "We the People of the United States," rather than merely on "we the states."

Done in Convention by the Unanimous Consent of the States present the Seventeenth Day of September in the Year of our Lord one thousand seven hundred and Eighty seven and of the Independence of the United States of America the Twelfth. In Witness whereof We have hereunto subscribed our Names.

Attest William Jackson, Secretary

Go. Washington, President and deputy from Virginia

☞ There were forty-one delegates present in the Assembly Room of the Pennsylvania State House on September 17, 1787. Thirty-eight of the delegates in the room signed the completed Constitution, with George Mason and Edmund Randolph of Virginia and Elbridge Gerry of Massachusetts refusing to add their assent. A forty-second delegate, John Dickinson of Delaware, had been suffering from debilitating headaches and went home a few days earlier, but he asked his Delaware colleague George Read to sign the document for him, bringing the total number of signatories to thirty-nine.

DELAWARE
Geo. Read
Gunning Bedford Jr.
John Dickinson
Richard Bassett
Jaco. Broom

MARYLAND
James McHenry
Dan of St. Thos. Jenifer
Danl. Carroll

VIRGINIA
John Blair
James Madison Jr.

NORTH CAROLINA
Wm. Blount
Richd. Dobbs Spaight
Hu Williamson

SOUTH CAROLINA
J. Rutledge
Charles Cotesworth Pinckney
Charles Pinckney
Pierce Butler

GEORGIA
William Few
Abr. Baldwin

NEW HAMPSHIRE
John Langdon
Nicholas Gilman

MASSACHUSETTS
Nathaniel Gorham
Rufus King

CONNECTICUT
Wm. Saml. Johnson
Roger Sherman

NEW YORK
Alexander Hamilton

NEW JERSEY
Wil. Livingston
David Brearley
Wm. Paterson
Jona. Dayton

PENNSYLVANIA
B. Franklin
Thomas Mifflin
Robt. Morris
Geo. Clymer
Thos. FitzSimons
Jared Ingersoll
James Wilson
Gouv. Morris

AMENDMENTS TO
THE CONSTITUTION

The framers of the original Constitution assumed that it was not necessary to include a "bill of rights" in their proposed plan for the union. The ostensible reason for the omission was that most of the state constitutions already possessed bills of rights, and therefore the inclusion of a bill of rights in the federal Constitution would be redundant. Another, more compelling reason may have been that when the idea of a bill of rights was raised in early September by Virginia delegate George Mason, the members of the Convention, tired and desperate to return home, feared that a debate on the subject might extend their stay in Philadelphia by many weeks, if not months.

The omission of a bill of rights proved to be both a tactical and strategic error. When the Constitution was submitted to the states for ratification, many of the critics of the Constitution pointed to the absence of a bill of rights as a fatal flaw in the document. As a consequence, the supporters of the Constitution, who called themselves Federalists, came forward with a promise to make the drafting of a bill of rights the first item of business when the new Congress convened after the ratification of the Constitution. On September 25, 1789, Congress presented to the states twelve amendments, ten of which received the necessary approval of three-quarters of the states on December 15, 1791. It is those ten amendments that are commonly referred to as the Bill of Rights. One of the two amendments not approved, dealing with congressional representation, has not proved of any significance in the operation of the Constitution. The other, dealing with congressional salaries, was eventually incorporated into the Twenty-seventh Amendment.

AMENDMENT I (1791)

Congress shall make no law respecting an establishment of religion, or prohibiting the free exercise thereof; or abridging the freedom of speech, or of the press; or the right of the people peaceably to assemble, and to petition the Government for a redress of grievances.

☞ The First Amendment is remarkably brief considering the breadth of protection that it has provided. The section of the amendment prohibiting Congress from making any law "respecting an establishment of religion" is a cornerstone of the American notion of separation of church and state, and the guarantee of "free exercise" of religion has proven a powerful means by which people have been allowed to express their religious beliefs without fear of government reprisal. Similarly, the guarantees of freedom of speech, of the press, and of the "right of the people peaceably to assemble," as well as the right to petition their government (and by implication to protest the actions of that government) are at the heart of the American constitutional definition of liberty.

Those freedoms have, however, been subject to some restrictions. Until the early twentieth century, the First Amendment applied only to the actions of the federal government; state governments were free to pass their own laws contravening some of the provisions of the First Amendment. For example, the state of Massachusetts continued to accord the Congregational Church special privileges and did not move to explicitly separate church and state until 1833. Moreover, throughout the nineteenth century, and sometimes into the twentieth, state governments have enacted laws placing restrictions on speech, freedom of the press, and on certain forms of public assembly. It was only in the twentieth century, through application of the "incorporation doctrine," that the Fourteenth Amendment's guarantee that states must not "abridge the privileges or immunities of citizens of the United States," nor deny citizens "equal protection of the laws," began to obligate state governments to guaran-

tee their residents the same freedoms as those articulated in the First Amendment.

The precise extent of the guarantees of the First
Amendment continues to be a subject of contention.
Oliver Wendell Holmes, in a Supreme Court opinion in
Schenck v. United States (1919), made the common-
sense argument that the guarantees of free speech do
not extend to the right to shout "fire in a theatre and
causing a panic" when no such danger actually exists.
Governments have often asserted the right to regulate
public assemblies and protests in order to ensure public safety.

Similarly, the "wall of separation" between church
and state is not impenetrable. The United States Congress continues to employ a chaplain, and the word of
God is frequently invoked at many official government
gatherings. The federal courts are frequently presented with cases in which litigants claim that public
displays of religious belief (e.g., the displaying of a Na-
tivity scene in a public square at Christmastime) vio-
late the principle of separation of church and state.
Thus far there is no clear resolution of where the
boundary between a religious and a civic display lies.

AMENDMENT II (1791)

A well regulated Militia, being necessary to the security of a free State, the right of the people to keep and
bear Arms, shall not be infringed.

☞ The Second Amendment contains two parts: a preface, which states that a "well regulated Militia" (meaning a citizens' army authorized by the state) is a necessary and desirable thing, and the operative section of the amendment, which asserts the right of the people to keep and bear arms. Constitutional scholars have argued vociferously about whether the comma separating those two parts signifies that the right to keep and bear arms without state interference is confined to the use of such arms in conjunction with one's duties as part of a government-sanctioned militia or army, or whether there is an individual right to keep and bear arms under any circumstances. The most recent rulings of the Supreme Court (*District of Columbia v. Heller*, 2008, and *McDonald v. Chicago*, 2010) suggest that the Second Amendment does guarantee an individual, as well as a collective, right to bear arms, but the Court has also conceded that there are some instances (e.g., regulating the sale of assault weapons) in which local, state, and federal governments do have the right to regulate the sale and use of arms.

AMENDMENT III (1791)

No Soldier shall, in time of peace be quartered in any house, without the consent of the Owner, nor in time of war, but in a manner to be prescribed by law.

☞ This amendment, which has lost much of its imme-
diacy over the course of time, was considered of pressing importance by the members of the First Congress,
who drafted it because attempts to force Americans to
provide lodgings for British troops (whom they considered to be hostile occupiers of their land) during the
years leading to the Revolution were an important
cause of that revolution. The amendment does, "in a
manner to be prescribed by law," allow the government
to use private homes to provide lodging for its own soldiers in time of war. More generally, the Third Amendment has—along with the Fourth, Fifth, and Ninth
Amendments—been interpreted to imply another right
not explicitly mentioned in the Constitution: the right
of privacy.

AMENDMENT IV (1791)

The right of the people to be secure in their persons,
houses, papers, and effects, against unreasonable
searches and seizures, shall not be violated, and no
Warrants shall issue, but upon probable cause, supported by Oath or affirmation, and particularly describing the place to be searched, and the persons or
things to be seized.

☞ The guarantees against "unreasonable searches and
seizures" of persons, houses, and property, and the insistence that any such searches be based on "probable

cause" and accompanied by search warrants, were another product of Americans' experience during the Revolution, when British customs officers and soldiers carried out blanket searches and seizures without proper warrants. In recent years, through use of the incorporation doctrine, the Fourth Amendment has been interpreted to mean that police officers at all levels of government must demonstrate probable cause before stopping and searching anyone whom they might suspect of a crime. The precise definition of "probable cause" has been much debated, and in many cases police officers are forced to make difficult judgments about whether they should detain an individual and search his or her possessions.

In an age in which advances in technology have offered the government new ways to gather evidence of a possible crime—e.g., GPS devices, CCTV cameras, and other means of sophisticated electronic surveillance— the federal courts have been presented with new dilemmas about how to interpret the provisions of the Fourth Amendment. Enactment of the Patriot Act in the aftermath of the 9/11 attacks in 2001 has significantly expanded the government's ability to carry out such surveillance.

AMENDMENT V (1791)

No person shall be held to answer for a capital, or otherwise infamous crime, unless on a presentment or indictment of a Grand Jury, except in cases arising in the land or naval forces, or in the Militia, when in actual service in time of War or public danger; nor shall any person be subject for the same offence to be twice put in jeopardy of life or limb; nor shall be compelled in any criminal case to be a witness against himself, nor be deprived of life, liberty, or property, without due process of law; nor shall private property be taken for public use, without just compensation.

Reflecting long-standing traditions of English common law, as well as the American perception that the British had violated those traditions in the years leading up to the American Revolution, the Fifth Amendment requires that people charged with capital crimes (i.e., a serious crime that falls under the jurisdiction of the federal courts) be first presented before a grand jury—a group of ordinary citizens drawn from the general population. Those serving in the military are not afforded that protection; they are to be tried in military courts, which set their own rules of judicial procedure.

Although indictment by a grand jury is standard practice in important civil and criminal proceedings at the federal level, many states have not used this mechanism for securing indictments of accused criminals, believing that grand juries are unnecessarily costly and time-consuming. Although many of the provisions of the Bill of Rights have been applied to the actions of state governments through the incorporation doctrine of the Fourteenth Amendment, the Supreme Court has not asserted that states are bound to conform to this particular provision of the Fifth Amendment.

The provision of the Fifth Amendment preventing double jeopardy stipulates that individuals cannot be tried for the same crime more than once. If a defendant is acquitted of a crime, the government does not have the right to prosecute that individual again, and if a defendant is convicted, the government may not impose multiple punishments for the same crime.

The phrase "taking the Fifth" refers to the provision of the Fifth Amendment ensuring the right against self-incrimination: the right to refuse to answer questions in court that might lead either to indictment or punishment for an alleged crime. Finally, the Fifth Amendment contains a very open-ended guarantee, echoing the words of the preamble of the Declaration of Independence, that no person can be deprived of the fundamental rights of life, liberty, or property without due process of law.

The concern for protection of property is further emphasized in the prohibition of the taking of private property for public use "without just compensation." In fact, federal and state governments have often taken control of private property (for example, for the purposes of building a highway or some other necessary public work) by using the doctrine of "eminent domain." In those cases, the owners are compensated for the value of their property, although in many cases not without significant litigation.

AMENDMENT VI (1791)

In all criminal prosecutions, the accused shall enjoy the right to a speedy and public trial, by an impartial jury of the State and district wherein the crime shall have been committed, which district shall have been previously ascertained by law, and to be informed of the nature and cause of the accusation; to be confronted with the witnesses against him; to have compulsory process for obtaining witnesses in his favor, and to have the Assistance of Counsel for his defence.

The Sixth Amendment is appropriately considered the centerpiece of the American criminal justice system. In addition to guaranteeing all criminal defendants a trial by jury, it provides an outline of the basic procedures to be followed in such trials. The trial shall be a speedy one, which is to say that accused criminals cannot be imprisoned for lengthy periods of time before receiving a trial. The trial must be public. The framers of the Sixth Amendment specifically rejected the format of English Star Chamber proceedings; that is, proceedings held in private, away from scrutiny by the public. The juries in criminal trials should, in normal instances, be drawn from ordinary citizens who are resident in the state and region where the crime was committed (although in unusual cases, if the crime is of such a sensational nature that it might prove impossible to impanel an *impartial* jury, the trial might be held in a jurisdiction other than the one in which the crime was committed).

The Sixth Amendment also guarantees to the accused the right to be confronted with the nature of the charges brought against him; the right to confront, either directly or through an attorney, the witnesses against him; and the right to present witnesses in his defense. Finally, criminal defendants are entitled to "Assistance of Counsel"; that is, a competent attorney to assist them in their defense. These basic guarantees have been elaborated in countless court cases in the more than two hundred years since the amendment was ratified and, through the incorporation doctrine, have become the standard procedure for criminal trials in states and other localities as well as in federal courts.

AMENDMENT VII (1791)

In Suits at common law, where the value in controversy shall exceed twenty dollars, the right of trial by jury shall be preserved, and no fact tried by a jury, shall be otherwise re-examined in any Court of the United States, than according to the rules of the common law.

The Seventh Amendment provides guarantees similar to those of the Sixth with respect to civil suits, although it does limit the right of trial by jury to suits in which there are substantial sums of money involved. The terms and extent of the application of this amendment have been worked out through myriad court cases involving plaintiffs (the person bringing the suit) and defendants (the person being sued). For example, while the standard for conviction in a criminal trial is a jury's unanimous verdict that the accused criminal is guilty "beyond a reasonable doubt," a jury in a civil case may award damages to a plaintiff if a majority of jurors find a "preponderance of evidence" on his or her behalf. The incorporation doctrine has not been applied to this amendment and, for the present, civil suits tried in state and local courts may follow different procedures from those outlined in the Seventh Amendment.

AMENDMENT VIII (1791)

Excessive bail shall not be required, nor excessive fines imposed, nor cruel and unusual punishments inflicted.

The prohibition against excessive bail (a sum of money put up to gain release from prison while awaiting a trial and returned if and when the accused appears for trial) is a reflection of the belief that an accused criminal is "presumed innocent until found guilty." The definition of "excessive bail" is a subjective one, but the intent of the amendment is to demand a sum of money sufficient to guarantee that the accused does show up for the trial, but not so high as to make it impossible for the accused to gain release.

The prohibition of "excessive fines" is intended to assure that "the punishment fits the crime." It is closely connected in its rationale with the final section of the amendment, the guarantee against "cruel and unusual punishments." Again drawing on English common law traditions, Americans were seeking to move away from ancient practices of gruesome punishments for relatively minor offenses. The definition of "cruel and unusual punishments" has often proven a point of contention. Currently, opponents of the death penalty argue that that punishment qualifies as cruel and unusual. Except for a period during the 1970s, the Supreme Court has not agreed, and both state governments and the federal government are free to permit executions if they desire (at present, thirty-five of the fifty states have laws permitting death penalties in some cases—usually, but not exclusively, murder cases).

AMENDMENT IX (1791)

The enumeration in the Constitution, of certain rights, shall not be construed to deny or disparage others retained by the people.

☞ One of the reasons given for the framers' omission of a Bill of Rights from the original Constitution was their fear that if they unintentionally failed to mention some fundamental rights in such a listing, those rights might go unprotected. That concern caused many of the delegates to fear that any debate over a bill of rights might drag on for weeks or months, as they sought to cover every conceivable right. The Ninth Amendment makes it clear that the list of rights mentioned in the Constitution and its amendments do not constitute all the possible rights to which the people are entitled. Over the years, the courts have defined "unenumerated" rights, such as the right to vote; the right to move about freely; and, perhaps most controversially, the right to privacy, including the right of a woman to have some control over her health and reproductive decisions.

AMENDMENT X (1791)

The powers not delegated to the United States by the Constitution, nor prohibited by it to the States, are reserved to the States respectively, or to the people.

☞ When the Constitution was presented for ratification to the people of the thirteen independent states, many were surprised—and alarmed—by the extent to which powers previously exercised by the states (for example, taxation and control over commerce) were now to be exercised by the federal government. In the words of Virginia statesman Patrick Henry, the new government was not really "federal" in character but rather a "consolidated government," one which would render the identity and powers of the states meaningless. The Tenth Amendment reserves all powers not specifically given to the federal government by the Constitution (most of which are contained in Article I, Section 8, in the enumeration of the powers of Congress) to the state governments; it was intended to allay fears about the federal government possessing excessive power.

In one sense, the Tenth Amendment is one of the most important features of the Constitution, for it articulates the principle that the federal government is one of specifically delegated powers, and that it should only exercise those powers explicitly enumerated in the Constitution. But in fact, the Tenth Amendment, because of its generality, has not proven to be much of an impediment to the steady expansion of federal power since the time the Constitution was adopted, although opponents of "big government" have in recent years invoked the Tenth Amendment in their arguments with greater frequency.

AMENDMENT XI (1795)

The Judicial power of the United States shall not be construed to extend to any suit in law or equity, commenced or prosecuted against one of the United States by Citizens of another State, or by Citizens or Subjects of any Foreign State.

✍️ In 1793 the Supreme Court ruled that it had a right to hear a suit brought by two citizens of South Carolina against the state of Georgia. Many members of Congress and of the state legislatures vigorously criticized the court's ruling, claiming that the federal courts had no business interfering with the "sovereign immunity" of state courts. The Eleventh Amendment reserved to the individual states the right to hear cases brought against them either by citizens of another state or another country. As is the case with many of the amendments to the Constitution, the Supreme Court has ruled that there are exceptions to this general rule. For example, since 1824 the Supreme Court has held that state government officials are not immune from being sued in a federal court if they act in violation of a right guaranteed by the U.S. Constitution.

AMENDMENT XII (1804)

The Electors shall meet in their respective states and vote by ballot for President and Vice-President, one of whom, at least, shall not be an inhabitant of the same state with themselves; they shall name in their ballots the person voted for as President, and in distinct ballots the person voted for as Vice-President, and they shall make distinct lists of all persons voted for as President, and of all persons voted for as Vice-President and of the number of votes for each, which lists they shall sign and certify, and transmit sealed to the seat of the government of the United States, directed to the President of the Senate.

The President of the Senate shall, in the presence of the Senate and House of Representatives, open all the certificates and the votes shall then be counted.

The person having the greatest Number of votes for President, shall be the President, if such number be a majority of the whole number of Electors appointed; and if no person have such majority, then from the persons having the highest numbers not exceeding three on the list of those voted for as President, the House of Representatives shall choose immediately, by ballot, the President. But in choosing the President, the votes shall be taken by states, the representation from each state having one vote; a quorum for this purpose shall consist of a member or members from two-thirds of the states, and a majority of all the states shall be necessary to a choice. And if the House of Representatives shall not choose a President whenever the right of choice shall devolve upon them, before the fourth day of March next following, then the Vice-President shall act as President, as in the case of the death or other constitutional disability of the President.

The person having the greatest number of votes as Vice-President, shall be the Vice-President, if such number be a majority of the whole number of Electors appointed, and if no person have a majority, then from the two highest numbers on the list, the Senate shall choose the Vice-President; a quorum for the purpose shall consist of two-thirds of the whole number of Senators, and a majority of the whole number shall be necessary to a choice. But no person constitutionally ineligible to the office of President shall be eligible to that of Vice-President of the United States.

☞ When the framers of the Constitution devised the complicated process by which presidential electors would select the nation's president and vice president, they assumed that those electors would run for their offices as individuals, and that the voters would select them on the basis of their individual merits. In that original notion of the way the electoral system would work, it was expected that the electors would each cast two ballots, with no distinction between a presidential and a vice-presidential ballot, and that the person receiving the greatest number of votes would be elected president and the person receiving the next largest number of votes vice president.

The framers of the Constitution did not anticipate the emergence of an organized political party system in which two extra-constitutional political parties, the Federalists and Jeffersonian Republicans, would organize electors (or, in some states, slates of electors) pledged in advance to vote for presidential and vice-presidential candidates as part of a party "ticket." In the election of 1800, the party ticket of Thomas Jefferson (the person whom the Republicans intended as their presidential candidate) and Aaron Burr (the person whom the Republicans intended as their vice-presidential candidate) received a majority of electoral votes. In fact, though, party discipline was so great that the electors cast their votes on their two ballots in such a way that Jefferson and Burr had an equal number of votes, with no constitutional mechanism for deciding which of the candidates was intended to be the presidential candidate and which the vice-presidential candidate. As a consequence, the election was thrown into the House of Representatives, where, after a great deal of intrigue, Jefferson was selected as president and Burr the vice president.

The adoption of the Twelfth Amendment was a necessary adjustment to the way in which the American party system had transformed America's presidential elections. Although the provisions of the Twelfth Amendment are as mind-numbingly complicated as the original provisions of Article II, Section 1, the essential feature of the amendment was that henceforth electors would vote separately for the president and vice president. And while the original language in Article II, Section 1, stipulated that the House of Representatives would choose among the five leading candidates should no one receive a majority of electoral votes, the new provision in the Twelfth Amendment narrowed the choice to the top three candidates.

AMENDMENT XIII (1865)
SECTION 1

Neither slavery nor involuntary servitude, except as a punishment for crime whereof the party shall have been duly convicted, shall exist within the United States, or any place subject to their jurisdiction.

SECTION 2

Congress shall have power to enforce this article by appropriate legislation.

☞ The Thirteenth Amendment was passed by Congress in 1861, as the Southern states were seceding from the union, but not ratified until 1865, after the South had accepted defeat in the Civil War. It marked the first important step in bringing American constitutional practice into harmony with American libertarian values. Although there had been previous, private attempts to eliminate slavery, usually accompanied by promises of compensation for the value of the "property" lost as a consequence of the emancipation of slaves, the Thirteenth Amendment unequivocally abolished slavery, providing for the immediate emancipation of all slaves in the United States, without compensation to their owners. It also gave to Congress the power to enforce the emancipation of slaves, a power that it exercised in the Civil Rights Act of 1866.

AMENDMENT XIV (1868)
SECTION 1

All persons born or naturalized in the United States, and subject to the jurisdiction thereof, are citizens of the United States and of the State wherein they reside. No State shall make or enforce any law which shall abridge the privileges or immunities of citizens of the United States; nor shall any State deprive any person of life, liberty, or property, without due process of law; nor deny to any person within its jurisdiction the equal protection of the laws.

SECTION 2

Representatives shall be apportioned among the several States according to their respective numbers, counting the whole number of persons in each State, excluding Indians not taxed. But when the right to vote at any election for the choice of electors for President and Vice-President of the United States, Representatives in Congress, the Executive and Judicial officers of a State, or the members of the Legislature thereof, is denied to any of the male inhabitants of such State, being twenty-one years of age, and citizens of the United States, or in any way abridged, except for participation in rebellion, or other crime, the basis of representation therein shall be reduced in the proportion which the number of such male citizens shall bear to the whole number of male citizens twenty-one years of age in such State.

SECTION 3

No person shall be a Senator or Representative in Congress, or elector of President and Vice-President, or hold any office, civil or military, under the United States, or under any State, who, having previously taken an oath, as a member of Congress, or as an officer of the United States, or as a member of any State legislature, or as an executive or judicial officer of any State, to support the Constitution of the United States, shall have engaged in insurrection or rebellion against the same, or given aid or comfort to the enemies thereof. But Congress may by a vote of two-thirds of each House, remove such disability.

SECTION 4

The validity of the public debt of the United States, authorized by law, including debts incurred for payment of pensions and bounties for services in suppressing insurrection or rebellion, shall not be questioned. But neither the United States nor any State shall assume or pay any debt or obligation incurred in aid of insurrection or rebellion against the United States, or any claim for the loss or emancipation of any slave; but all such debts, obligations and claims shall be held illegal and void.

SECTION 5

The Congress shall have power to enforce, by appropriate legislation, the provisions of this article.

Perhaps the most significant and far-reaching amendment to the Constitution, the Fourteenth Amendment is viewed by many scholars and jurists as the provision of the Constitution that has brought the principles enunciated in the preamble of the Declaration of Independence into the realm of constitutional law. The words of the preamble of the Declaration— "that all men are created equal, that they are endowed by their Creator with certain unalienable Rights, that among these are Life, Liberty and the pursuit of Happiness"—are purely exhortatory; they were important rhetorically in defining American purposes as they declared the colonies' independence from Great Britain, but they do not have the force of law. At the heart of the Fourteenth Amendment is the stipulation that all Americans born or naturalized in the United States, including the newly freed slaves, are citizens of the United States, and that no state may make or enforce any law that shall infringe on the rights of American citizens, including those unalienable rights of "life, liberty or property" without due process of law. The Fourteenth Amendment's promise that all persons are guaranteed "equal protection of the laws" would prove an important mechanism by which the Supreme Court, in a series of rulings in the twentieth century, would articulate a uniform standard by which many of the rights spelled out in the Bill of Rights would be guaranteed to all citizens in each of the states.

Section 2 of the Fourteenth Amendment had a more specific intent. It effectively repealed the three-fifths compromise by which slaves were counted as three-fifths of a person in the apportionment of representation and taxation, and stipulates that any state that attempts to deny the right to vote to any male United States citizen over the age of twenty-one will have its representation in Congress and the electoral college reduced proportionally to the number of citizens so disenfranchised. This part of Section 2 was clearly intended by the members of Congress who drafted it as a means of protecting the newly freed slaves' right to vote. It is notable that the only exception to this protection of the right to vote is in the case of individuals who have participated "in rebellion, or other crime." This exception not only applied to convicted criminals (who are still denied the right to vote in most states) but also to large numbers of Americans who had participated in the Southern "rebellion" during the Civil War.

Section 3 of the amendment explicitly excluded former Southern rebels from serving in any federal or state office until Congress, by a two-thirds vote, removed that prohibition. This constitutional device effectively turned over control of the "reconstruction" of the former secessionist states to individuals who had remained loyal to the union during the Civil War.

Section 4 of the amendment absolved the federal government of any responsibility for the debts incurred by the Southern states or by the Confederacy during the Civil War.

Finally, Section 5 granted to Congress broad authority to proceed with legislation that would enforce the provisions of the Fourteenth Amendment. In the immediate aftermath of the adoption of the amendment, Congress passed seven statutes aimed at guaranteeing civil rights to freed slaves as well as imposing conditions for readmission to the union on the states that had seceded from it. Over the course of the next two decades, many of the provisions of those statutes would be ruled unconstitutional by the Supreme Court, which adopted an increasingly narrow interpretation of the rights granted by the Fourteenth Amendment.

AMENDMENT XV (1870)
SECTION I

The right of citizens of the United States to vote shall not be denied or abridged by the United States or by any State on account of race, color, or previous condition of servitude.

SECTION 2

The Congress shall have the power to enforce this article by appropriate legislation.

☞ While the Fourteenth Amendment punished states that deprived newly freed slaves of the right to vote by reducing their representation in the House of Representatives, the Fifteenth Amendment categorically prohibits the denial of the right to vote on account of race, color, or previous condition of servitude. Notably, the amendment does not mention gender, which, to the dismay of advocates of women's suffrage, meant that although newly freed male slaves were guaranteed a right to vote, women of all races were denied that right. In spite of the adoption of the Fifteenth Amendment, the states of the former Confederacy managed to find ways to continue to drastically curtail the right of African Americans to vote, through the use of poll taxes, literacy tests, and other discriminatory devices. It was not until the passage of the Voting Rights Act of 1965 that African Americans have had equal access to the polling place.

AMENDMENT XVI (1913)

The Congress shall have power to lay and collect taxes on incomes, from whatever source derived, without apportionment among the several States, and without regard to any census or enumeration.

🖘 Although the original version of the Constitution gave Congress the power to levy direct taxes, such taxation was only to be levied on the states themselves, in direct proportion to their population. Although Congress during the Civil War was able to levy a direct tax on individuals as part of a wartime measure, the Supreme Court, in an 1895 ruling (*Pollock v. Farmers Loan and Trust Co.*), ruled that taxing the property of individuals was unconstitutional. The Sixteenth Amendment effectively reversed that ruling. It is silent on what the rate of taxation might be (for example, it does not speak to whether all individuals should be taxed at an equal rate or whether the rate of taxation should be progressively higher on higher incomes). Congress, which enacted a federal income tax law in October 1913, just seven months after the passage of the Sixteenth Amendment, opted for a modestly progressive tax rate. The rate of taxation imposed on the top taxation bracket has varied from 7 percent in 1913 to a high of 92 percent in 1952–53. The current rate of taxation in the top bracket is 38.6 percent, nearer the low end of that continuum.

AMENDMENT XVII (1913)

The Senate of the United States shall be composed of two Senators from each State, elected by the people thereof, for six years; and each Senator shall have one vote. The electors in each State shall have the qualifications requisite for electors of the most numerous branch of the State legislatures.

When vacancies happen in the representation of any State in the Senate, the executive authority of such State shall issue writs of election to fill such vacancies: *Provided*, That the legislature of any State may empower the executive thereof to make temporary appointments until the people fill the vacancies by election as the legislature may direct.

This amendment shall not be so construed as to affect the election or term of any Senator chosen before it becomes valid as part of the Constitution.

When the Constitution was first drafted, the framers believed that the Senate, the upper house, should be the repository of superior wisdom and virtue and, toward that end, stipulated that senators should be elected by the legislatures of each of the states, whose members would presumably be able to make a wiser choice than the people at large. As one of a series of reforms during the Progressive Era, Congress proposed, and the states endorsed, an amendment calling for direct, popular election of senators.

AMENDMENT XVIII (1919)
SECTION I

After one year from the ratification of this article the manufacture, sale, or transportation of intoxicating liquors within, the importation thereof into, or the exportation thereof from the United States and all territory subject to the jurisdiction thereof for beverage purposes is hereby prohibited.

SECTION 2

The Congress and the several States shall have concurrent power to enforce this article by appropriate legislation.

SECTION 3

This article shall be inoperative unless it shall have been ratified as an amendment to the Constitution by the legislatures of the several States, as provided in the Constitution, within seven years from the date of the submission hereof to the States by the Congress.

☞ Most of the amendments to the Constitution seek to grant specific rights to the people by placing restraints on the actions of the government. The Eighteenth Amendment is the only amendment that has sought to restrict the rights of the people—in this case the right to manufacture, sell, or transport "intoxicating liquors" within the United States. Interestingly, it does not prevent the consumption of liquor. Though liquor consumption declined markedly during the years when the amendment was in force, it certainly did not cease. Indeed, as people turned to illegal sources for their alcoholic beverages, the operation of the Eighteenth Amendment served to encourage otherwise law-abiding people to break the law and bolster the activities of organized crime.

AMENDMENT XIX (1920)

The right of citizens of the United States to vote shall not be denied or abridged by the United States or by any State on account of sex.

Congress shall have power to enforce this article by appropriate legislation.

☞ The Nineteenth Amendment was the culmination of more than three-quarters of a century of dedicated work by advocates of female suffrage. Although some states had passed legislation allowing women the right to vote prior to 1920, that right was not extended to all women until the adoption of the Nineteenth Amendment. Unlike the operation of the Fifteenth Amendment, which was thwarted by states that found ways to continue to deny the vote to African Americans, the amendment granting women the right to vote encountered little resistance in the aftermath of its passage.

AMENDMENT XX (1933)
SECTION 1

The terms of the President and Vice President shall end at noon on the 20th day of January, and the terms of Senators and Representatives at noon on the 3d day of January, of the years in which such terms would have ended if this article had not been ratified; and the terms of their successors shall then begin.

SECTION 2

The Congress shall assemble at least once in every year, and such meeting shall begin at noon on the 3d day of January, unless they shall by law appoint a different day.

SECTION 3

If, at the time fixed for the beginning of the term of the President, the President elect shall have died, the Vice President elect shall become President. If a President shall not have been chosen before the time fixed for the beginning of his term, or if the President elect shall have failed to qualify, then the Vice President elect shall act as President until a President shall have qualified; and the Congress may by law provide for the case wherein neither a President elect nor a Vice President elect shall have qualified, declaring who shall then act as President, or the manner in which one who is to act shall be selected, and such person shall act accordingly until a President or Vice President shall have qualified.

SECTION 4

The Congress may by law provide for the case of the death of any of the persons from whom the House of Representatives may choose a President whenever the right of choice shall have devolved upon them, and for the case of the death of any of the persons from whom the Senate may choose a Vice President whenever the right of choice shall have devolved upon them.

SECTION 5

Sections 1 and 2 shall take effect on the 15th day of October following the ratification of this article.

SECTION 6

This article shall be inoperative unless it shall have been ratified as an amendment to the Constitution by the legislatures of three-fourths of the several States within seven years from the date of its submission.

☞ Many of the most consequential amendments to the Constitution (e.g., the first ten amendments) are remarkably brief, while some of the more arcane amendments seem to require more elaborate verbiage. This is certainly the case with the Twentieth Amendment.

Traditionally, new presidents took office in March, creating a significant time gap between their election in November and their inauguration. In some cases, this time lag had serious consequences. For example, during the period between Abraham Lincoln's election and inauguration, his Democratic predecessor, James Buchanan, found himself to be a lame-duck president at a time when Southern states were seceding from the union. In recognition of the improvements in communication and transportation since the Constitution was originally adopted, the Twentieth Amendment reduced the amount of time elapsing between the president's election and his inauguration. It also moved the meeting time of a newly elected Congress from March to January 3, preventing the meeting of a lame-duck session of Congress whose actions might not be consonant with the will of the electorate as expressed in the November elections.

The remaining parts of the Twentieth Amendment seek to clarify the role of Congress in determining a plan of succession in case of the death or removal of both the president and vice president. For much of the nineteenth century, Congress designated the president pro tempore of the Senate as next in line of succession;

from the 1880s until 1947, Congress stipulated that the secretary of state would be next in line. The decision to change the law and provide for the Speaker of the House to assume office in case of the president and vice president's absence was shaped by the desire to have a popularly elected official—in this case the leader of the legislative branch most directly responsible to the people—assume the presidency.

AMENDMENT XXI (1933)
SECTION I

The eighteenth article of amendment to the Constitution of the United States is hereby repealed.

SECTION 2

The transportation or importation into any State, Territory, or Possession of the United States for delivery or use therein of intoxicating liquors, in violation of the laws thereof, is hereby prohibited.

SECTION 3

The article shall be inoperative unless it shall have been ratified as an amendment to the Constitution by conventions in the several States, as provided in the Constitution, within seven years from the date of the submission hereof to the States by the Congress.

☞ Just as the Eighteenth Amendment is the only constitutional amendment to restrict the rights of the American people, the Twenty-first Amendment, which ended Prohibition, is the only amendment in the Constitution to repeal a previous amendment. The Twenty-first Amendment does not specifically allow for the manufacture, transport, or sale of liquors but, rather, returns to the states the right to regulate alcohol distribution and consumption. This amendment is unusual in that it specifies that state conventions, rather than state legislatures, should be the bodies responsible for ratifying the amendment.

AMENDMENT XXII (1951)
SECTION 1

No person shall be elected to the office of the President more than twice, and no person who has held the office of President, or acted as President, for more than two years of a term to which some other person was elected President shall be elected to the office of President more than once. But this Article shall not apply to any person holding the office of President when this Article was proposed by the Congress, and shall not prevent any person who may be holding the office of President, or acting as President, during the term within which this Article becomes operative from holding the office of President or acting as President during the remainder of such term.

SECTION 2

This article shall be inoperative unless it shall have been ratified as an amendment to the Constitution by the legislatures of three-fourths of the several States within seven years from the date of its submission to the States by the Congress.

☞ Although the people of the United States had expressed their will by electing Franklin D. Roosevelt president in four successive elections, in the aftermath of Roosevelt's terms in office many Americans began to have second thoughts about the wisdom of allowing a president to exceed what had previously been the "two-term tradition" set by George Washington. By the terms of the Twenty-second Amendment, Presidents are limited to two terms, or if they have served at least two years of a previous president's term, to one term. Americans continue to disagree on whether "term limits"—either in the executive or legislative branches—are consistent with democratic governance, and there have been occasional attempts to repeal the Twenty-second Amendment, although none has come close to success thus far.

AMENDMENT XXIII (1961)
SECTION 1

The District constituting the seat of Government of the United States shall appoint in such manner as the Congress may direct:

A number of electors of President and Vice President equal to the whole number of Senators and Representatives in Congress to which the District would be entitled if it were a State, but in no event more than the least populous State; they shall be in addition to those appointed by the States, but they shall be considered, for the purposes of the election of President and Vice President, to be electors appointed by a State; and they shall meet in the District and perform such duties as provided by the twelfth article of amendment.

SECTION 2

The Congress shall have power to enforce this article by appropriate legislation.

The District of Columbia, seat of the nation's government, has always occupied a peculiar place within our federal system. The Constitution empowered Congress to designate a territory "not exceeding ten Miles square" as the nation's capital but specifically intended that the "federal district" not be within the boundaries or jurisdiction of any particular state. Therefore, while the federal government exercises much of its enormous power within the District of Columbia, that territory has been denied voting representatives in Congress, and until the passage of the Twenty-third Amendment, its residents were denied the right to vote in presidential elections. By the terms of the Twenty-third Amendment the residents of the District of Columbia are entitled to vote for presidential electors, with the number of electors representing the district being equal to the number of senators and representatives that the district would have if it were a state. On the basis of its present population, that means three electors.

AMENDMENT XXIV (1964)
SECTION I

The right of citizens of the United States to vote in any primary or other election for President or Vice President, for electors for President or Vice President, or for Senator or Representative in Congress, shall not be denied or abridged by the United States or any State by reason of failure to pay any poll tax or other tax.

SECTION 2

The Congress shall have power to enforce this article by appropriate legislation.

🖙 Although the Fourteenth and Fifteenth Amendments were intended to ensure African Americans the right to vote, the imposition of a poll tax—a fee that citizens had to pay to the state or locality if they wished to vote—was a common device by which states, particularly those in the South, prevented low-income voters, who were often predominantly African American, from voting. The Twenty-fourth Amendment explicitly prohibits the imposition of taxes as a condition for voting. The amendment does not say anything about the use of the poll tax in state elections, but soon after the passage of the Twenty-fourth Amendment, the Supreme Court, citing the "equal protection" clause of the Fourteenth Amendment, ruled that it was unconstitutional for states to require the payment of poll taxes as a condition for voting in state elections.

AMENDMENT XXV (1967)
SECTION 1

In case of the removal of the President from office or of his death or resignation, the Vice President shall become President.

SECTION 2

Whenever there is a vacancy in the office of the Vice President, the President shall nominate a Vice President who shall take office upon confirmation by a majority vote of both Houses of Congress.

SECTION 3

Whenever the President transmits to the President pro tempore of the Senate and the Speaker of the House of Representatives his written declaration that he is unable to discharge the powers and duties of his office, and until he transmits to them a written declaration to the contrary, such powers and duties shall be discharged by the Vice President as Acting President.

SECTION 4

Whenever the Vice President and a majority of either the principal officers of the executive departments or of such other body as Congress may by law provide, transmit to the President pro tempore of the Senate and the Speaker of the House of Representatives their written declaration that the President is unable to discharge the powers and duties of his office, the Vice President shall immediately assume the powers and duties of the office as Acting President.

Thereafter, when the President transmits to the President pro tempore of the Senate and the Speaker of the House of Representatives his written declaration that no inability exists, he shall resume the powers and duties of his office unless the Vice President and a majority of either the principal officers of the executive department or of such other body as Congress may by law provide, transmit within four days to the President pro tempore of the Senate and the Speaker of the House of Representatives their written declaration that the President is unable to discharge the powers and duties of his office. Thereupon Congress shall decide the issue, assembling within forty-eight hours for that purpose if not in session. If the Congress, within twenty-one days after receipt of the latter written declaration, or, if Congress is not in session, within twenty-one days after Congress is required to assemble, determines by two-thirds vote of both Houses that the President is unable to discharge the powers and duties of his office, the Vice President shall continue to discharge the same as Acting President; otherwise, the President shall resume the powers and duties of his office.

☞ Although the Twentieth Amendment deals in part with the issue of presidential succession, the Twenty-fifth Amendment provides a more detailed description of how Congress should proceed in the event of the death or removal of a president or vice president, or in the case of the temporary disability of the president (for example, if the president falls seriously ill or undergoes an operation and is not able for a period of time to exercise the duties of his office). Eight American presidents have died in office, and one has resigned. And there have been several occasions when a president has been temporarily disabled (for example, when Ronald Reagan was wounded by a would-be assassin's bullet in 1985, he transferred power to his vice president, George H. W. Bush, while he was hospitalized).

The amendment also deals with the delicate question of how to deal with the disability of a president when the president himself is not willing to declare such a disability. For example, in 1918 President Woodrow Wilson suffered a stroke and many believed that his disability prevented him from carrying out the duties of his office effectively, but there were no means by which to resolve the issue. The Twenty-sixth Amendment stipulates that Congress may, if two-thirds of the members of both houses agree, provide written declaration that the president is disabled and then transfer power to the vice president.

AMENDMENT XXVI (1971)
SECTION I

The right of citizens of the United States, who are eighteen years of age or older, to vote shall not be denied or abridged by the United States or by any State on account of age.

SECTION 2

The Congress shall have power to enforce this article by appropriate legislation.

☞ It is no accident that this amendment giving citizens eighteen years or older the right to vote was passed at the height of the Vietnam War. Some of the reasoning behind the amendment was that if young men and women are old enough to serve and risk their lives in the military, then they should also be given the right to vote.

AMENDMENT XXVII (1992)

No law, varying the compensation for the services of the Senators and Representatives, shall take effect, until an election of Representatives shall have intervened.

☞ The Twenty-seventh Amendment was originally part of the package of twelve amendments submitted to the states by the First Congress in 1789, but it was not ratified at that time. Agitation to reconsider the amendment resurfaced in the 1980s, as the public became increasingly unhappy over a series of pay raises that members of Congress awarded themselves. The provisions of this amendment make it impossible for members of Congress to put into effect increases in their salaries before the session in which they are serving has ended. By this mechanism, members of Congress seeking reelection have to justify their proposed increases in salary to voters during their reelection campaigns.